CAMBRIDGE LIBRARY COLLECTION

Books of enduring scholarly value

English Men of Letters

In the 1870s, Macmillan publishers began to issue a series of books called 'English Men of Letters' – biographies of English writers by other English writers. The general editor of the series was the journalist, critic, politician, and supporter (and later biographer) of Gladstone, John Morley (1838–1923). The first volume published was Samuel Johnson, by Leslie Stephen (1878), and the first series (which continued until 1892) eventually consisted of 39 volumes. The aim was to provide a short introduction to each subject and his works, but also that the life should illuminate the works, and vice versa. All the subjects were men, as were all but one of the authors (Mrs Oliphant on Sheridan); and all but one (Hawthorne) were English or Irish. The subjects range chronologically from Chaucer to Thackeray and Dickens, and an important feature of the series is that many of the authors (Henry James on Hawthorne, Ward on Dickens) were discussing writers of the previous generation, and some (Trollope on Thackeray) had even known their subjects personally. The series exemplifies the British approach to literary biography and criticism at the end of the nineteenth century, and also reveals which authors were at that time regarded as canonical.

Spenser

Edmund Spenser (1552–99) has been described as one of the greatest English poets, and is best known for *The Faerie Queene*, which he composed in celebration of the Tudor dynasty and Elizabeth I. Published in the first series of English Men of Letters in 1879, this biography by R. W. Church (1815–90), Dean of St Paul's, recounts Spenser's life and work, hailing him as a genius who continued the Chaucerian tradition of reflecting the deepest human passions through verse. Beginning with an account of his early life and his time as a Cambridge scholar, Church moves on to explore Spenser's career as secretary to Lord Grey of Wilton, the then Lord Deputy of Ireland. He concludes with a detailed analysis of *The Faerie Queene*, explaining its significance as a work of moral philosophy, and one that represented a cornerstone of English literary history.

T0382392

Cambridge University Press has long been a pioneer in the reissuing of out-of-print titles from its own backlist, producing digital reprints of books that are still sought after by scholars and students but could not be reprinted economically using traditional technology. The Cambridge Library Collection extends this activity to a wider range of books which are still of importance to researchers and professionals, either for the source material they contain, or as landmarks in the history of their academic discipline.

Drawing from the world-renowned collections in the Cambridge University Library, and guided by the advice of experts in each subject area, Cambridge University Press is using state-of-the-art scanning machines in its own Printing House to capture the content of each book selected for inclusion. The files are processed to give a consistently clear, crisp image, and the books finished to the high quality standard for which the Press is recognised around the world. The latest print-on-demand technology ensures that the books will remain available indefinitely, and that orders for single or multiple copies can quickly be supplied.

The Cambridge Library Collection will bring back to life books of enduring scholarly value (including out-of-copyright works originally issued by other publishers) across a wide range of disciplines in the humanities and social sciences and in science and technology.

Spenser

RICHARD WILLIAM CHURCH

CAMBRIDGE UNIVERSITY PRESS

Cambridge, New York, Melbourne, Madrid, Cape Town,
Singapore, São Paolo, Delhi, Tokyo, Mexico City

Published in the United States of America by Cambridge University Press, New York

www.cambridge.org
Information on this title: www.cambridge.org/9781108034739

This edition first published 1879
This digitally printed version 2011

ISBN 978-1-108-03473-9 Paperback

English Men of Letters

EDITED BY JOHN MORLEY

SPENSER

SPENSER

BY

R. W. CHURCH,

DEAN OF ST. PAUL'S,

HONORARY FELLOW OF ORIEL COLLEGE.

London:

MACMILLAN AND CO.

1879

NOTICE.

As the plan of these volumes does not encourage foot-notes, I wish to say that, besides the biographies prefixed to the various editions of Spenser, there are two series of publications, which have been very useful to me. One is the series of Calendars of State Papers, especially the State Papers on Ireland and the Carew MSS. at Lambeth, with the prefaces of Mr. Hans Claude Hamilton and the late Professor Brewer. The other is Mr. E. Arber's series of reprints of old English books, and his Transcript of the Stationers' Registers, a work, I suppose, without parallel in its information about the early literature of a country, and edited by him with admirable care and public spirit. I wish also to say that I am much indebted to Mr. Craik's excellent little book on *Spenser and his Poetry.*

R. W. C.

March, 1879.

CONTENTS.

CHAPTER I.

SPENSER'S EARLY LIFE (1552—1579) 1

PAGE

CHAPTER II.

THE NEW POET—THE SHEPHERD'S CALENDAR (1579) . . 29

CHAPTER III.

SPENSER IN IRELAND (1580) 51

CHAPTER IV.

THE FAERY QUEEN—THE FIRST PART (1580—1590) . . 81

CHAPTER V.

THE FAERY QUEEN 118

CHAPTER VI.

SECOND PART OF THE FAERY QUEEN—SPENSER'S LAST
YEARS (1590—1599) 166

SPENSER.

CHAPTER I.

[1552—1579.]

SPENSER marks a beginning in English literature. He is
the first Englishman who, in that great division of our
history which dates from the Reformation, attempted and
achieved a poetical work of the highest order. Born about
the same time as Hooker (1552—1554), in the middle
of that eventful century which began with Henry VIII.,
and ended with Elizabeth, he was the earliest of our great
modern writers in poetry, as Hooker was the earliest of our
great modern writers in prose. In that reviving English
literature, which, after Chaucer's wonderful promise, had
been arrested in its progress, first by the Wars of the Roses,
and then by the religious troubles of the Reformation,
these two were the writers who first realized to Englishmen
the ideas of a high literary perfection. These ideas
vaguely filled many minds; but no one had yet shown the
genius and the strength to grasp and exhibit them in a
way to challenge comparison with what had been accomplished by the poetry and prose of Greece Rome, and

B

Italy. There had been poets in England since Chaucer,
and prose writers since Wycliffe had translated the Bible.
Surrey and Wyatt have deserved to live, while a crowd of
poets, as ambitious as they, and not incapable of occasional
force and sweetness, have been forgotten. Sir Thomas
More, Roger Ascham, Tyndale, the translator of the New
Testament, Bishop Latimer, the writers of many state
documents, and the framers, either by translation or com
position, of the offices of the English Prayer Book, showed
that they understood the power of the English language
over many of the subtleties and difficulties of thought, and
were alive to the music of its cadences. Some of these
works, consecrated by the highest of all possible associations, have remained, permanent monuments and standards
of the most majestic and most affecting English speech.
But the verse of Surrey, Wyatt, and Sackville, and the
prose of More and Ascham were but noble and promising
efforts. Perhaps the language was not ripe for their success ; perhaps the craftsmen's strength and experience were
not equal to the novelty of their attempt. But no one can
compare the English styles of the first half of the sixteenth
century with the contemporary styles of Italy, with Ariosto,
Machiavelli, Guicciardini, without feeling the immense
gap in point of culture, practice, and skill—the immense
distance at which the Italians were ahead, in the finish and
reach of their instruments, in their power to handle them,
in command over their resources, and facility and ease in
using them. The Italians were more than a century older ;
the English could not yet, like the Italians, say what they
would ; the strength of English was, doubtless, there in
germ, but it had still to reach its full growth and develop-
ment. Even the French prose of Rabelais and Montaigne
was more mature. But in Spenser, as in Hooker, all these

tentative essays of vigorous but unpractised minds have led
up to great and lasting works. We have forgotten all these
preliminary attempts, crude and imperfect, to speak with
force and truth, or to sing with measure and grace. There
is no reason why they should be remembered, except by
professed inquirers into the antiquities of our literature;
they were usually clumsy and awkward, sometimes
grotesque, often affected, always hopelessly wanting in the
finish, breadth, moderation, and order which alone can
give permanence to writing. They were the necessary
exercises by which Englishmen were recovering the
suspended art of Chaucer, and learning to write;
and exercises, though indispensably necessary, are not
ordinarily in themselves interesting and admirable. But
when the exercises had been duly gone through, then arose
the original and powerful minds, to take full advantage of
what had been gained by all the practising, and to concentrate and bring to a focus all the hints and lessons of art
which had been gradually accumulating. Then the sustained strength and richness of the *Faery Queen* became
possible; contemporary with it, the grandeur and force
of English prose began in Hooker's *Ecclesiastical Polity;*
and then, in the splendid Elizabethan Drama, that form
of art which has nowhere a rival, the highest powers
of poetic imagination became wedded, as they had never
been before in England or in the world, to the real
facts of human life, and to its deepest thoughts and
passions.

More is known about the circumstances of Spenser's life
than about the lives of many men of letters of that time;
yet our knowledge is often imperfect and inaccurate. The
year 1552 is now generally accepted as the year of his
birth. The date is inferred from a passage in one of his

Sonnets,[1] and this probably is near the truth. That is
to say that Spenser was born in one of the last two years
of Edward VI.; that his infancy was passed during the
dark days of Mary; and that he was about six years old
when Elizabeth came to the throne. About the same
time were born Ralegh, and, a year or two later (1554),
Hooker and Philip Sidney. Bacon (1561), and Shakespere (1564), belong to the next decade of the century.

He was certainly a Londoner by birth, and early training. This also we learn from himself, in the latest poem
published in his life-time. It is a bridal ode (*Prothalamion*), to celebrate the marriage of two daughters of the
Earl of Worcester, written late in 1596. It was a time
in his life of disappointment and trouble, when he was
only a rare visitor to London. In the poem he imagines
himself on the banks of London's great river, and the
bridal procession arriving at Lord Essex's house; and he
takes occasion to record the affection with which he still
regarded "the most kindly nurse" of his boyhood.

> Calm was the day, and through the trembling air
> Sweet-breathing Zephyrus did softly play,
> A gentle spirit, that lightly did delay
> Hot Titan's beams, which then did glister fair:
> When I, (whom sullen care,
> Through discontent of my long fruitless stay
> In Princes Court, and expectation vain
> Of idle hopes, which still do fly away,
> Like empty shadows, did afflict my brain,)
> Walkt forth to ease my pain

---

[1] ——Since the winged god his planet clear
Began in me to move, one year is spent:
The which doth longer unto me appear
Than *all those forty* which my life outwent.
Sonnet LX., probably written in 1593 or 1594.

Along the shore of silver-streaming Thames ;
Whose rutty bank, the which his river hems,
Was painted all with variable flowers,
And all the meads adorned with dainty gems
Fit to deck maidens' bowers,
And crown their paramours
Against the bridal day, which is not long:
Sweet Thames ! run softly, till I end my song.

     *   *   *   *   •

At length they all to merry London came,
To merry London, my most kindly nurse,
That to me gave this life's first native source,
Though from another place I take my name,
A house of ancient fame.
There, when they came, whereas those bricky towers
The which on Thames broad aged back do ride,
Where now the studious lawyers have their bowers,
There whilome wont the Templar Knights to bide,
Till they decayed through pride :
Next whereunto there stands a stately place,
Where oft I gained gifts and goodly grace [2]
Of that great Lord, which therein wont to dwell ;
Whose want too well now feels my friendless case ;
But ah ! here fits not well
Old woes, but joys, to tell
Against the bridal day, which is not long :
Sweet Thames ! run softly, till I end my song :
Yet therein now doth lodge a noble peer,[3]
Great England's glory and the wide world's wonder,
Whose dreadful name late through all Spain did thunder,
And Hercules two pillars, standing near,
Did make to quake and fear.
Fair branch of honour, flower of chivalry !
That fillest England with thy triumph's fame,
Joy have thou of thy noble victory,[4]
And endless happiness of thine own name
That promiseth the same.

---

[2] Leicester House, then Essex House, in the Strand.
[3] Earl of Essex.   [4] At Cadiz, June 21, 1596.

> That through thy prowess, and victorious arms,
> Thy country may be freed from foreign harms ;
> And great Elisa's glorious name may ring
> Through all the world, filled with thy wide alarms.

Who his father was, and what was his employment we
know not. From one of the poems of his later years we
learn that his mother bore the famous name of Elizabeth,
which was also the cherished one of Spenser's wife.

> My love, my life's best ornament,
> By whom my spirit out of dust was raised.

But his family, whatever was his father's condition,
certainly claimed kindred, though there was a difference
in the spelling of the name, with a house then rising into
fame and importance, the Spencers of Althorpe, the
ancestors of the Spencers and Churchills of modern days.
Sir John Spencer had several daughters, three of whom
made great marriages. Elizabeth was the wife of Sir
George Carey, afterwards the second Lord Hunsdon, the
son of Elizabeth's cousin and Counsellor. Anne, first,
Lady Compton, afterwards married Thomas Sackville, the
son of the poet, Lord Buckhurst, and then Earl of Dorset.
Alice, the youngest, whose first husband, Lord Strange,
became Earl of Derby, after his death married Thomas
Egerton, Lord Keeper, Baron Ellesmere, and then Viscount
Brackley. These three sisters are celebrated by him in
a gallery of the noble ladies of the Court,[6] under poetical
names—" Phyllis, the flower of rare perfection," "Cha-
rillis, the pride and primrose of the rest," and " Sweet
Amaryllis, the youngest but the highest in degree."

---

[5] *Sonnet* LXXIV.
[6] *Colin Clout's come Home again*, l. 536. Craik, *Spenser*,
i. 9. 10.

Alice, Lady Strange, Lady Derby, Lady Ellesmere and
Brackley, and then again Dowager Lady Derby, the " Sweet
Amaryllis " of the poet, had the rare fortune to be a
personal link between Spenser and Milton. She was
among the last whom Spenser honoured with his homage :
and she was the first whom Milton honoured; for he
composed his Arcades to be acted before her by her
grandchildren, and the *Masque of Comus* for her son-
in-law, Lord Bridgewater, and his daughter, another Lady
Alice.   With these illustrious sisters Spenser claimed
kindred.   To each of these he dedicated one of his minor
poems ; to Lady Strange, the *Tears of the Muses;* to Lady
Compton, the Apologue of the Fox and the Ape, *Mother
Hubberd's Tale ;* to Lady Carey, the Fable of the Butterfly
and the Spider, *Muiopotmos.*   And in each dedication he
assumed on their part the recognition of his claim.

> The sisters three,
> The honour of the noble family,
> Of which I meanest boast myself to be.

Whatever his degree of relationship to them, he could
hardly even in the days of his fame have ventured thus
publicly to challenge it, unless there had been some acknowledged ground for it.   There are obscure indications, which
antiquarian diligence may perhaps make clear, which
point to East Lancashire as the home of the particular
family of Spensers to which Edmund Spenser's father
belonged.   Probably he was, however, in humble circumstances.

Edmund Spenser was a Londoner by education as well
as birth. A recent discovery by Mr. R. B. Knowles, further
illustrated by Dr. Grosart,[7] has made us acquainted with

---

[7] See *The Spending of the Money of Robert Nowell,* 1568—1580 :

Spenser's school. He was a pupil, probably one of the
earliest ones, of the grammar school, then recently (1560)
established by the Merchant Taylors' Company, under a
famous teacher, Dr. Mulcaster. Among the manuscripts
at Townley Hall are preserved the account books of the
executors of a bountiful London citizen, Robert Nowell,
the brother of Dr. Alexander Nowell, who was Dean of
St. Paul's during Elizabeth's reign, and was a leading
person in the ecclesiastical affairs of the time. In these
books, in a crowd of unknown names of needy relations
and dependents, distressed foreigners, and parish paupers,
who shared from time to time the liberality of Mr.
Robert Nowell's representatives, there appear among the
numerous "poor scholars" whom his wealth assisted, the
names of Richard Hooker, and Lancelot Andrewes. And
there, also, in the roll of the expenditure at Mr. Nowell's
pompous funeral at St. Paul's in February, 156$\frac{8}{9}$, among
long lists of unknown men and women, high and low,
who had mourning given them, among bills for fees to
officials, for undertakers' charges, for heraldic pageantry
and ornamentation, for abundant supplies for the sump-
tuous funeral banquet, are put down lists of boys, from the
chief London schools, St. Paul's, Westminster, and others,
to whom two yards of cloth were to be given to make
their gowns : and at the head of the six scholars named
from Merchant Taylors' is the name of Edmund Spenser.

He was then, probably, the senior boy of the school,
and in the following May he went to Cambridge. The
Nowells still helped him : we read in their account books
under April 28, 1569, " to Edmond Spensore, scholler of
the m'chante tayler scholl, at his gowinge to penbrocke

from the MSS. at Towneley Hall. Edited by Rev. A. B. Grosart.
1877.

hall in chambridge, xˢ." On the 20th of May, he was
admitted sizar, or serving clerk at Pembroke Hall; and on
more than one occasion afterwards, like Hooker and like
Lancelot Andrewes, also a Merchant Taylors' boy, two
or three years Spenser's junior, and a member of the same
college, Spenser had a share in the benefactions, small in
themselves, but very numerous, with which the Nowells
after the fine fashion of the time, were accustomed to
assist poor scholars at the Universities. In the visitations of Merchant Taylors' School, at which Grindal,
Bishop of London, was frequently present,[8] it is not un-
likely that his interest was attracted, in the appositions
or examinations, to the promising senior boy of the school.
At any rate Spenser, who afterwards celebrated Grindal's
qualities as a bishop, was admitted to a place, one which
befitted a scholar in humble circumstances, in Grindal's
old college. It is perhaps worth noticing that all Spenser's
early friends, Grindal, the Nowells, Dr. Mulcaster, his
master, were north country men.

Spenser was sixteen or seventeen when he left school for
the university, and he entered Cambridge at the time when
the struggle which was to occupy the reign of Elizabeth
was just opening. At the end of the year 1569, the first
distinct blow was struck against the queen and the new
settlement of religion, by the Rising of the North. In the
first ten years of Elizabeth's reign, Spenser's school time
at Merchant Taylors', the great quarrel had slumbered.
Events abroad occupied men's minds; the religious wars
in France, the death of the Duke of Guise (1563), the
loss of Havre, and expulsion of the English garrisons, the
close of the Council of Trent (1563), the French peace,

---

[8] H. B. Wilson, *Hist. of Merchant Taylors' School*, p. 23.

the accession of Pius V. (156⅝). Nearer home, there
was the marriage of Mary of Scotland with Henry Darnley
(1565), and all the tragedy which followed, Kirk of Field
(1567), Lochleven, Langside, Carlisle, the imprisonment
of the pretender to the English Crown (1568). In England, the authority of Elizabeth had established itself, and
the internal organization of the Reformed Church was
going on, in an uncertain and tentative way, but steadily.
There was a struggle between Genevan exiles, who were
for going too fast, and bishops and politicians who were
for going too slow; between authority and individual
judgment, between home-born state traditions and foreign
revolutionary zeal. But outwardly, at least, England had
been peaceful. Now however a great change was at
hand. In 1566, the Dominican Inquisitor, Michael Ghis-
lieri, was elected Pope, under the title of Pius V.

In Pius (1566-72), were embodied the new spirit and
policy of the Roman Church, as they had been created
and moulded by the great Jesuit order, and by reforming
bishops like Ghiberti of Verona, and Carlo Borromeo of
Milan. Devout and self-denying as a saint, fierce and
inflexible against abuses as a puritan, resolute and uncompromising as a Jacobin idealist or an Asiatic despot,
ruthless and inexorable as an executioner, his soul was
bent on re-establishing, not only by preaching and martyr-
dom, but by the sword and by the stake, the unity of
Christendom and of its belief. Eastwards and westwards,
he beheld two formidable foes and two serious dangers;
and he saw before him the task of his life in the heroic
work of crushing English heresy and beating back
Turkish misbelief. He broke through the temporizing
caution of his predecessors by the Bull of Deposition
against Elizabeth in 1570. He was the soul of the con-

federacy which won the day of Lepanto against the
Ottomans in 1571. And though dead, his spirit was
paramount in the slaughter of St. Bartholomew in 1572.

In the year 1569, while Spenser was passing from school
to college, his emissaries were already in England, spread-
ing abroad that Elizabeth was a bastard and an apostate,
incapable of filling a Christian throne, which belonged by
right to the captive Mary. The seed they sowed bore
fruit. In the end of the year, southern England was
alarmed by the news of the rebellion of the two great
Earls in the north, Percy of Northumberland and Neville
of Westmoreland. Durham was sacked and the mass
restored by an insurgent host, before which an "aged
gentleman," Richard Norton with his sons, bore the
banner of the Five Wounds of Christ. The rebellion was
easily put down, and the revenge was stern. To the men
who had risen at the instigation of the Pope and in the
cause of Mary, Elizabeth gave, as she had sworn "such
a breakfast as never was in the North before." The
hangman finished the work on those who had escaped
the sword. Poetry, early and late, has recorded the
dreary fate of those brave victims of a mistaken cause,
in the ballad of the *Rising of the North,* and in the
White Doe of Rylstone. It was the signal given for the
internecine war which was to follow between Rome and
Elizabeth. And it was the first great public event which
Spenser would hear of in all men's mouths, as he entered on
manhood, the prelude and augury of fierce and dangerous
years to come. The nation awoke to the certainty—one
which so profoundly affects sentiment and character both
in a nation and in an individual—that among the
habitual and fixed conditions of life is that of having a
serious and implacable enemy ever to reckon with.

And in this year, apparently in the transition time between school and college, Spenser's literary ventures began.
The evidence is curious, but it seems to be clear. In 1569,
a refugee Flemish physician from Antwerp, who had fled
to England from the "abominations of the Roman Anti-
christ" and the persecutions of the Duke of Alva, John
Vander Noodt, published one of those odd miscellanies,
fashionable at the time, half moral and poetical, half
fiercely polemical, which he called a " *Theatre*, wherein
be represented as well the Miseries and Calamities which
follow the voluptuous Worldlings, as also the great Joys
and Pleasures which the Faithful do enjoy—an argument
both profitable and delectable to all that sincerely love
the word of God." This "little treatise," was a mixture
of verse and prose, setting forth in general, the vanity of
the world, and, in particular, predictions of the ruin of
Rome and Antichrist: and it enforced its lessons by
illustrative woodcuts. In this strange jumble are preserved, we can scarcely doubt, the first compositions
which we know of Spenser's. Among the pieces are some
Sonnets of Petrarch, and some Visions of the French
poet Joachim du Bellay, whose poems were published
in 1568. In the collection itself, these pieces are said
by the compiler to have been translated by him "out of
the Brabants speech," and "out of Dutch into English."
But in a volume of "poems of the world's vanity," and
published years afterwards in 1591, ascribed to Spenser,
and put together, apparently with his consent, by his
publisher, are found these very pieces from Petrarch
and Du Bellay. The translations from Petrarch are
almost literally the same, and are said to have been
"formerly translated." In the Visions of Du Bellay
there is this difference, that the earlier translations are in

blank verse, and the later ones are rimed as sonnets ; but
the change does not destroy the manifest identity of the two
translations. So that unless Spenser's publisher, to whom
the poet had certainly given some of his genuine pieces
for the volume, is not to be trusted,—which, of course,
is possible, but not probable—or unless,—what is in the
last degree inconceivable,—Spenser had afterwards been
willing to take the trouble of turning the blank verse of
Du Bellay's unknown translator into rime, the Dutchman
who dates his *Theatre of Worldlings* on the 25th May,
1569, must have employed the promising and fluent
school boy, to furnish him with an English versified
form, of which he himself took the credit, for compositions which he professes to have known only in the
Brabants or Dutch translations. The sonnets from Petrarch are translated with much command of language ;
there occurs in them, what was afterwards a favourite
thought of Spenser's :—

> —The Nymphs,
> That sweetly in accord did *tune their voice*
> *To the soft sounding of the waters' fall.*[9]

It is scarcely credible that the translator of the sonnets
could have caught so much as he has done of the
spirit of Petrarch without having been able to read
the Italian original ; and if Spenser was the translator,
it is a curious illustration of the fashionableness of Italian
literature in the days of Elizabeth, that a school-boy just
leaving Merchant Taylors' should have been so much
interested in it. Dr. Mulcaster, his master, is said by
Warton to have given special attention to the teaching of
the English language.

If these translations were Spenser's, he must have

9 Comp. *Sheph. Cal.* April 1. 36. June 1. 8. F. Q. 6. 10. 7.

gone to Cambridge with a faculty of verse, which for
his time may be compared to that with which winners
of prize poems go to the universities now. But there
was this difference, that the school-boy versifiers of our
days are rich with the accumulated experience and
practice of the most varied and magnificent poetical
literature in the world; while Spenser had but one
really great English model behind him; and Chaucer,
honoured as he was, had become in Elizabeth's time, if not
obsolete, yet in his diction, very far removed from the
living language of the day. Even Milton, in his boyish
compositions, wrote after Spenser and Shakespere, with
their contemporaries, had created modern English poetry.
Whatever there was in Spenser's early verses of grace
and music was of his own finding : no one of his own
time, except in occasional and fitful snatches, like stanzas
of Sackville's, had shown him the way. Thus equipped,
he entered the student world, then full of pedantic and
ill-applied learning, of the disputations of Calvinistic
theology, and of the beginnings of those highly specula-
tive puritanical controversies, which were the echo at the
University of the great political struggles of the day, and
were soon to become so seriously practical. The University was represented to the authorities in London as
being in a state of dangerous excitement, troublesome
and mutinous. Whitgift, afterwards Elizabeth's favourite
archbishop, Master, first of Pembroke, and then of Trinity,
was Vice-Chancellor of the University; but as the
guardian of established order, he found it difficult to
keep in check the violent and revolutionary spirit of the
theological schools. Calvin was beginning to be set up
there as the infallible doctor of Protestant theology.
Cartwright from the Margaret Professor's chair was teach-

ing the exclusive and divine claims of the Geneva platform of discipline, and in defiance of the bishops and
the government was denouncing the received Church
polity and ritual as Popish and anti-Christian. Cartwright, an extreme and uncompromising man, was de-
prived in 1570; but the course which things were taking
under the influence of Rome and Spain gave force to his
lessons and warnings, and strengthened his party. In this
turmoil of opinions, amid these hard and technical debates,
these fierce conflicts between the highest authorities, and
this unsparing violence and bitterness of party recrimina-
tions, Spenser, with the tastes and faculties of a poet, and
the love not only of what was beautiful, but of what was
meditative and dreamy, began his university life.

It was not a favourable atmosphere for the nurture of
a great poet. But it suited one side of Spenser's mind, as
it suited that of all but the most independent Englishmen
of the time, Shakespere, Bacon, Ralegh. Little is known
of Spenser's Cambridge career. It is probable, from the persons with whom he was connected, that he would not be
indifferent to the debates around him, and that his religious
prepossessions were then, as afterwards, in favour of the con-
forming puritanism in the Church, as opposed to the extreme
and thorough-going puritanism of Cartwright. Of the con-
forming puritans, who would have been glad of a greater
approximation to the Swiss model, but who, whatever
their private wishes or dislikes, thought it best, for good
reasons or bad, to submit to the strong determination of
the government against it, and to accept what the government approved and imposed, Grindal, who held successively
the great sees of London, York, and Canterbury, and
Nowell, Dean of St. Paul's, Spenser's benefactor, were
representative types. Grindal, a waverer like many others

in opinion, had also a noble and manly side to his character, in his hatred of practical abuses, and in the courageous
and obstinate resistance which he could offer to power, when
his sense of right was outraged.   Grindal, as has been said,
was perhaps instrumental in getting Spenser into his own
old college, Pembroke Hall, with the intention, it may be,
as was the fashion of bishops of that time, of becoming
his patron.   But certainly after his disgrace in 1577, and
when it was not quite safe to praise a great man under the
displeasure of the Court, Grindal is the person whom Spenser
first singled out for his warmest and heartiest praise.   He is
introduced under a thin disguise, "Algrind," in Spenser's
earliest work after he left Cambridge, the *Shepherd's Calendar*, as the pattern of the true and faithful Christian pastor.
And if Pembroke Hall retained at all the tone and tendencies of such masters as Ridley, Grindal, and Whitgift,
the school in which Spenser grew up was one of their
mitigated puritanism.   But his puritanism was political
and national, rather than religious.   He went heartily
with the puritan party in their intense hatred of Rome
and Roman partisans; he went with them also in their
denunciations of the scandals and abuses of the ecclesiastical government at home.   But in temper of mind
and intellectual bias he had little in common with
the puritans.   For the stern austerities of Calvinism, its
fierce and eager scholasticism, its isolation from human
history, human enjoyment, and all the manifold play and
variety of human character, there could not be much
sympathy in a man like Spenser, with his easy and
flexible nature, keenly alive to all beauty, an admirer
even when he was not a lover of the alluring pleasures of
which the world is full, with a perpetual struggle going
on in him, between his strong instincts of purity and

right, and his passionate appreciation of every charm
and grace. He shows no signs of agreement with the
internal characteristics of the puritans, their distinguishing theology, their peculiarities of thought and habits,
their protests, right or wrong, against the fashions
and amusements of the world. If not a man of pleasure, he yet threw himself without scruple into the
tastes, the language, the pursuits, of the gay and gallant
society in which they saw so much evil: and from
their narrow view of life, and the contempt, dislike, and
fear, with which they regarded the whole field of human
interest, he certainly was parted by the widest gulf.
Indeed, he had not the sternness and concentration of
purpose, which made Milton the great puritan poet.

Spenser took his Master's degree in 1576, and then left
Cambridge. He gained no Fellowship, and there is
nothing to show how he employed himself. His classical
learning, whether acquired there or elsewhere, was
copious, but curiously inaccurate; and the only specimen
remaining of his Latin composition in verse is con-
temptible in its mediæval clumsiness. We know nothing
of his Cambridge life except the friendships which he
formed there. An intimacy began at Cambridge of the
closest and most affectionate kind, which lasted long
into after-life, between him and two men of his college,
one older in standing than himself, the other younger;
Gabriel Harvey, first a fellow of Pembroke, and then a
student or teacher of civil law at Trinity Hall, and
Edward Kirke, like Spenser, a sizar at Pembroke, recently
identified with the E. K., who was the editor and commentator of Spenser's earliest work, the anonymous *Shepherd's Calendar*. Of the younger friend this is the most
that is known. That he was deeply in Spenser's con-

fidence as a literary coadjutor, and possibly in other ways,
is shown in the work which he did.   But Gabriel Harvey
was a man who had influence on Spenser's ideas and purposes, and on the direction of his efforts.   He was a
classical scholar of much distinction in his day, well read
in the Italian authors then so fashionable, and regarded as
a high authority on questions of criticism and taste.
Except to students of Elizabethan literary history, he has
become an utterly obscure personage; and he has not
usually been spoken of with much respect.   He had the
misfortune, later in life, to plunge violently into the
scurrilous quarrels of the day, and as he was matched with
wittier and more popular antagonists, he has come down
to us as a foolish pretender, or at least as a dull and
stupid scholar who knew little of the real value of the
books he was always ready to quote, like the pedant of the
comedies, or Shakespere's schoolmaster Holofernes.   Further, he was one who, with his classical learning, had
little belief in the resources of his mother tongue, and he
was one of the earliest and most confident supporters of a
plan then fashionable, for reforming English verse, by
casting away its natural habits and rhythms, and imposing
on it the laws of the classical metres.   In this he was not
singular.   The professed treatises of this time on poetry, of
which there were several, assume the same theory, as the
mode of "reforming" and duly elevating English verse.   It
was eagerly accepted by Philip Sidney and his Areopagus
of wits at court, who busied themselves in devising rules
of their own—improvements as they thought on those of
the university men—for English hexameters and sapphics,
or as they called it, artificial versifying.   They regarded
the comparative value of the native English rhythms and
the classical metres, much as our ancestors of Addison's

day regarded the comparison between Gothic and Palladian
architecture. One, even if it sometimes had a certain
romantic interest, was rude and coarse; the other was the
perfection of polite art and good taste. Certainly in what
remains of Gabriel Harvey's writing, there is much that
seems to us vain and ridiculous enough; and it has been
naturally surmised that he must have been a dangerous
friend and counsellor to Spenser. But probably we are
hard upon him. His writings, after all, are not much more
affected and absurd in their outward fashion than most of
the literary composition of the time; his verses are no
worse than those of most of his neighbours; he was not
above, but he was not below, the false taste and clumsiness
of his age; and the rage for "artificial versifying" was for
the moment in the air. And it must be said, that though
his enthusiasm for English hexameters is of a piece with
the puritan use of scripture texts in divinity and morals,
yet there is no want of hard-headed shrewdness in his
remarks; indeed, in his rules for the adaptation of English
words and accents to classical metres, he shows clearness
and good sense in apprehending the conditions of the problem, while Sidney and Spenser still appear confused and
uncertain. But in spite of his pedantry, and though he
had not, as we shall see, the eye to discern at first the
genius of the *Faery Queen*, he has to us the interest of
having been Spenser's first, and as far as we can see, to
the last, dearest friend. By both of his younger fellow-
students at Cambridge, he was looked up to with the
deepest reverence, and the most confiding affection. Their
language is extravagant, but there is no reason to think
that it was not genuine. E. Kirke, the editor of Spenser's
first venture, the *Shepherd's Calendar*, commends the
"new poet" to his patronage, and to the protection

of his "mighty rhetoric," and exhorts Harvey himself to seize the poetical "garland which to him alone is due." Spenser speaks in the same terms; "*veruntamen te sequor solum; nunquam vero assequar.*" Portions of the early correspondence between Harvey and Spenser have been preserved to us, possibly by Gabriel Harvey's self-satisfaction in regard to his own compositions. But with the pedagogue's jocoseness, and a playfulness which is like that of an elephant, it shows on both sides easy frankness, sincerity, and warmth, and not a little of the early character of the younger man. In Spenser's earliest poetry, his pastorals, Harvey appears among the imaginary rustics, as the poet's "special and most familiar friend," under the name of Hobbinol,—

> "Good Hobbinol, that was so true."

To him Spenser addresses his confidences, under the name of Colin Clout, a name borrowed from Skelton, a satirical poet of Henry VIII.'s time, which Spenser kept throughout his poetical career. Harvey reappears in one of Spenser's latest writings, a return to the early pastoral, *Colin Clout's come home again*, a picture drawn in distant Ireland, of the brilliant but disappointing court of Elizabeth. And from Ireland in 1586, was addressed to Harvey by "his devoted friend during life," the following fine sonnet, which, whatever may have been the merit of Harvey's criticisms and his literary quarrels with Greene and Nash, shows at least Spenser's unabated honour for him.

To the Right Worshipful, my singular good Friend, M. Gabriel Harvey, Doctor of the Laws.

> Harvey, the happy above happiest men
> I read; that, sitting like a looker on
> Of this world's stage, dost note with critic pen
> The sharp dislikes of each condition;

And, as one careless of suspicion,
Ne fawnest for the favour of the great ;
Ne fearest foolish reprehension
Of faulty men, which danger to thee threat ;
But freely dost, of what thee list, entreat,
Like a great lord of peerless liberty ;
Lifting the good up to high honour's seat,
And the evil damning ever more to die ;
For life and death is in thy doomful writing ;
So thy renown lives ever by enditing.

Dublin, this xviii. of July, 1586.   Your devoted friend, during life,
                                        EDMUND SPENSER.

Between Cambridge and Spenser's appearance in London, there is a short but obscure interval. What is certain is, that he spent part of it in the North of England ;
that he was busy with various poetical works, one of which
was soon to make him known as a new star in the poetical
heaven ; and lastly, that in the effect on him of a deep
but unrequited passion, he then received what seems to
have been a strong and determining influence on his
character and life. It seems likely that his sojourn in
the north, which perhaps first introduced the London-bred
scholar, the "Southern Shepherd's Boy," to the novel and
rougher country life of distant Lancashire, also gave form
and local character to his first considerable work. But we
do not know for certain where his abode was in the north ;
of his literary activity, which must have been considerable,
we only partially know the fruit ; and of the lady whom
he made so famous, that her name became a consecrated
word in the poetry of the time, of Rosalind, the " Widow's
Daughter of the Glen," whose refusal of his suit, and pre-
ference for another, he lamented so bitterly, yet would
allow no one else to blame, we know absolutely nothing.
She would not be his wife ; but apparently, he never
ceased to love her through all the chances and temptations, and possibly errors of his life, even apparently in

the midst of his passionate admiration of the lady whom,
long afterwards, he did marry. To her kindred and condition, various clues have been suggested, only to provoke
and disappoint us. Whatever her condition, she was
able to measure Spenser's powers : Gabriel Harvey has
preserved one of her compliments—" Gentle Mistress
Rosalind once reported him to have all the intelligences
at commandment ; and at another, christened him her
Signior Pegaso." But the unknown Rosalind had given
an impulse to the young poet's powers, and a colour to his
thoughts, and had enrolled Spenser in that band and order
of poets,—with one exception, not the greatest order,—to
whom the wonderful passion of love, in its heights and
its depths, is the element on which their imagination
works, and out of which it moulds its most beautiful and
characteristic creations.

But in October, 1579, he emerges from obscurity. If
we may trust the correspondence between Gabriel Harvey
and Spenser, which was published at the time, Spenser
was then in London.[1] It was the time of the crisis of the
Alençon courtship, while the Queen was playing fast and
loose with her Valois lover, whom she playfully called her
frog ; when all about her, Burghley, Leicester, Sidney,
and Walsingham, were dismayed, both at the plan itself,
and at her vacillations ; and just when the Puritan pamphleteer, who had given expression to the popular disgust
at a French marriage, especially at a connexion with the
family which had on its hands the blood of St. Bartholomew, was sentenced to lose his right hand as a seditious

---

[1] Published in June, 1580. Reprinted incompletely in Haslewood, *Ancient Critical Essays* (1815), ii. 255. Extracts given in
editions of Spenser by Hughes, Todd, and Morris. The letters
are of April, 1579, and October, 1580.

libeller. Spenser had become acquainted with Philip
Sidney, and Sidney's literary and courtly friends. He
had been received into the household of Sidney's uncle,
Lord Leicester, and dates one of his letters from Leicester
House. Among his employments he had written, " *Stemmata Dudleiana*." He is doubting whether or not to
publish, " to utter," some of his poetical compositions : he
is doubting, and asks Harvey's advice, whether or not to
dedicate them to His Excellent Lordship, " lest by our
much cloying their noble ears he should gather contempt of
myself, or else seem rather for gain and commodity to do
it, and some sweetness that I have already tasted." Yet,
he thinks, that when occasion is so fairly offered of esti-
mation and preferment, it may be well to use it : " while
the iron is hot, it is good striking ; and minds of nobles
vary, as their estates." And he was on the eve of starting
across the sea to be employed in Leicester's service, on
some permanent mission in France, perhaps in connexion
with the Alençon intrigues. He was thus launched into
what was looked upon as the road of preferment ; in his
case, as it turned out, a very subordinate form of public
employment, which was to continue almost for his lifetime.
Sidney had recognized his unusual power, if not yet his
genius. He brought him forward ; perhaps he accepted
him as a friend. Tradition makes him Sidney's com-
panion at Penshurst ; in his early poems, Kent is the
county with which he seems most familiar. But Sidney
certainly made him known to the queen ; he probably
recommended him as a promising servant to Leicester :
and he impressed his own noble and beautiful character
deeply on Spenser's mind. Spenser saw and learned in
him what was then the highest type of the finished
gentleman. He led Spenser astray. Sidney was not

without his full share of that affectation, which was then thought refinement. Like Gabriel Harvey, he induced Spenser to waste his time on the artificial versifying which was in vogue. But such faults and mistakes of fashion, and in one shape or another they are inevitable in all ages, were as nothing, compared to the influence on a highly receptive nature, of a character so elevated and pure, so genial, so brave and true. It was not in vain that Spenser was thus brought so near to his "Astrophel."

These letters tell us all that we know of Spenser's life at this time. During these anxious eighteen months, and connected with persons like Sidney and Leicester, Spenser only writes to Harvey on literary subjects. He is discreet, and will not indulge Harvey's "desire to hear of my late being with her Majesty." According to a literary fashion of the time, he writes and is addressed as *M. Immerito*, and the great business which occupies him and fills the letters is the scheme devised in Sidney's *Areopagus* for the "general surceasing and silence of bald Rymers, and also of the very best of them too; and for prescribing certain laws and rules of quantities of English syllables for English verse." Spenser "is more in love with his English versifying than with ryming,"—"which," he says to Harvey, "I should have done long since, if I would then have followed your counsel." Harvey, of course, is delighted; he thanks the good angel which puts it into the heads of Sidney and Edward Dyer, "the two very diamonds of her Majesty's court," "our very Castor and Pollux," to "help forward our new famous enterprise for the exchanging of barbarous rymes for artificial verses;" and the whole subject is discussed at great length between the two friends; "Mr. Drant's" rules are compared with those of "Mr. Sidney," revised by "Mr. Immerito;" and

examples, highly illustrative of the character of the
"famous enterprise" are copiously given. In one of Harvey's letters we have a curious account of changes of
fashion in studies and ideas at Cambridge. They seem
to have changed since Spenser's time.

I beseech you all this while, what news at *Cambridge?*
Tully and *Demosthenes* nothing so much studied as they were
wont: *Livy* and *Sallust* perhaps more, rather than less:
Lucian never so much: *Aristotle* much named but little read:
Xenophon and *Plato* reckoned amongst discoursers, and con-
ceited superficial fellows; much verbal and sophistical jangling;
little subtle and effectual disputing. *Machiavel* a great man:
Castilio, of no small repute: *Petrarch* and *Boccace* in every
man's mouth: *Galateo* and *Guazzo* never so happy: but some
acquainted with *Unico Aretino:* the *French* and *Italian*
highly regarded: the *Latin* and *Greek* but lightly. The *Queen
Mother* at the beginning or end of every conference: all in-
quisitive after news: new *books,* new fashions, new laws, new
officers, and some after new elements, some after new heavens
and hells too. *Turkish* affairs familiarly known: castles built
in the air: much ado, and little help: in no age so little so
much made of; every one highly in his own favour. Something
made of nothing, in spight of Nature: numbers made of cyphers,
in spight of Art. Oxen and asses, notwithstanding the absurdity
it seemed to *Plautus,* drawing in the same yoke: the Gospel
taught, not learnt; Charity cold; nothing good, but by impu-
tation; the Ceremonial Law in word abrogated, the Judicial in
effect disannull'd, the Moral abandon'd; *the Light, the Light*
in every man's lips, but mark their eyes, and you will say they
are rather like owls than eagles. As of old books, so of ancient
virtue, honesty, fidelity, equity, new abridgments; every day
spawns new opinions: heresy in divinity, in philosophy, in
humanity, in manners, grounded upon hearsay; doctors con-
temn'd; the *devil* not so hated as the *pope;* many invectives,
but no amendment. No more ado about caps and surplices;
Mr. *Cartwright* quite forgotten.

      *   *   *   *   *

David, Ulysses, and *Solon,* feign'd themselves fools and madmen ; our fools and madmen feign themselves *Davids, Ulysses's,*
and *Solons.* It is pity fair weather should do any hurt ; but
I know what peace and quietness hath done with some melancholy pickstraws.

The letters preserve a good many touches of character
which are interesting. This, for instance, which shows
Spenser's feeling about Sidney. " New books," writes
Spenser, " I hear of none, but only of one, that writing
a certain book called *The School of Abuse,* [Stephen
Gosson's *Invective against poets, pipers, players, &c.*]
and dedicating to M. Sidney, was for his labour scorned :
if at least it be in the goodness of that nature to scorn."
As regards Spenser himself, it is clear from the letters that
Harvey was not without uneasiness lest his friend, from his
gay and pleasure-loving nature, and the temptations round
him, should be carried away into the vices of an age,
which, though very brilliant and high-tempered, was also
a very dissolute one. He couches his counsels mainly in
Latin ; but they point to real danger ; and he adds in
English,—" Credit me, I will never lin [=cease] baiting
at you, till I have rid you quite of this yonkerly and
womanly humour." But in the second pair of letters of
April, 1580, a lady appears. Whether Spenser was her
husband or her lover, we know not ; but she is his " sweetheart." The two friends write of her in Latin. Spenser
sends in Latin the saucy messages of his sweetheart,
"meum corculum," to Harvey ; Harvey, with academic
gallantry, sends her in Latin as many thanks for her
charming letter as she has hairs, "half golden, half silver,
half jewelled, in her little head ;"—she is a second little
Rosalind—"altera Rosalindula," whom he salutes as
"Domina Immerito, mea bellissima Colina Clouta." But

whether wife or mistress, we hear of her no more. Further, the letters contain notices of various early works of Spenser. The "new" *Shepherd's Calendar*, of which more will be said, had just been published. And in this correspondence of April, 1580, we have the first mention of the *Faery Queen*. The compositions here mentioned have been either lost, or worked into his later poetry; his *Dreams, Epithalamion Thamesis*, apparently in the "reformed verse," his *Dying Pelican*, his *Slumber*, his *Stemmata Dudleiana*, his *Comedies*. They show at least the activity and eagerness of the writer in his absorbing pursuit. But he was still in bondage to the belief that English poetry ought to try to put on a classical dress. It is strange that the man who had written some of the poetry in the *Shepherd's Calendar* should have found either satisfaction or promise in the following attempt at Trimeter Iambics.

And nowe requite I you with the like, not with the verye beste, but with the verye shortest, namely, with a few Iambickes : I dare warrant they be precisely perfect for the feete (as you can easily judge), and varie not one inch from the Rule. I will imparte yours to Maister *Sidney* and Maister *Dyer* at my nexte going to the Courte. I praye you, keepe mine close to your selfe, or your verie entire friends, Maister *Preston*, Maister *Still*, and the reste.

Iambicum Trimetrum.

Unhappie Verse, the witnesse of my unhappie state,
  Make thy selfe fluttring wings of thy fast flying
  Thought, and fly forth unto my Love wheresoever she be :

Whether lying reastlesse in heavy bedde, or else
  Sitting so cheerlesse at the cheerfull boorde, or else
  Playing alone carelesse on hir heavenlie Virginals.

If in Bed, tell hir, that my eyes can take no reste :
If at Boorde, tell hir that my mouth can eate no meate :
If at hir Virginals, tell hir, I can heare no mirth.

Asked why ? say : Waking Love suffereth no sleepe :
Say, that raging Love dothe appall the weake stomacke :
Say, that lamenting Love marreth the Musicall.

Tell hir, that hir pleasures were wonte to lull me asleepe :
Tell hir, that hir beautie was wonte to feede mine eyes :
Tell hir, that hir sweete Tongue was wonte to make me mirth.

Nowe doe I nightly waste, wanting my kindely reste :
Nowe doe I dayly starve, wanting my lively foode :
Nowe doe I alwayes dye, wanting thy timely mirth.

And if I waste, who will bewaile my heavy chaunce ?
And if I starve, who will record my cursed end ?
And if I dye, who will saye : *this was Immerito ?*

CHAPTER II.

[1579.]

It is clear that when Spenser appeared in London, he had found out his powers and vocation as a poet. He came from Cambridge, fully conscious of the powerful attraction of the imaginative faculties, conscious of an extraordinary command over the resources of language, and with a singular gift of sensitiveness to the grace and majesty and suggestiveness of sound and rhythm, such as makes a musician. And whether he knew it or not, his mind was in reality made up, as to what his English poetry was to be. In spite of opinions and fashions round him, in spite of university pedantry and the affectations of the court, in spite of Harvey's classical enthusiasm, and Sidney's Areopagus, and in spite of half-fancying himself converted to their views, his own powers and impulses showed him the truth, and made him understand better than his theories what a poet could and ought to do with English speech in its free play and genuine melodies. When we first come upon him, we find that at the age of twenty-seven, he had not only realized an idea of English poetry far in advance of anything which his age had yet conceived or seen; but that, besides what he had executed or planned, he had already in his mind the outlines of

the *Faery Queen,* and, in some form or other, though
perhaps not yet as we have it, had written some portion
of it.

In attempting to revive for his own age Chaucer's suspended art, Spenser had the tendencies of the time with
him. The age was looking out for some one to do for
England what had been grandly done for Italy. The time
in truth was full of poetry. The nation was just in that
condition which is most favourable to an outburst of
poetical life or art. It was highly excited; but it was
also in a state of comparative peace and freedom from exter-
nal disturbance. "An over-faint quietness," writes Sidney
in 1581, lamenting that there were so few good poets,
"should seem to strew the house for poets." After the
first ten years of Elizabeth's reign, and the establishment
of her authority, the country had begun to breathe freely,
and fall into natural and regular ways. During the first
half of the century, it had had before it the most
astonishing changes which the world had seen for centuries. These changes seemed definitely to have run
their course; with the convulsions which accompanied
them, their uprootings and terrors, they were gone; and
the world had become accustomed to their results. The
nation still had before it great events, great issues, great
perils, great and indefinite prospects of adventure and
achievement. The old quarrels and animosities of Europe
had altered in character : from being wars between princes,
and disputes of personal ambition, they had attracted into
them all that interests and divides mankind, from high
to low. Their animating principle was a high and a sacred
cause : they had become wars of liberty, and wars of
religion. The world had settled down to the fixed
antipathies and steady rivalries of centuries to come. But

the mere shock of transition was over. Yet the remembrance of the great break-up was still fresh. For fifty years the English people had had before its eyes the great vicissitudes which make tragedy. They had seen the most unforeseen and most unexpected revolutions in what had for ages been held certain and immovable; the overthrow of the strongest institutions, and most venerable authorities; the violent shifting of feelings from faith to passionate rejection, from reverence to scorn and a hate which could not be satisfied. They had seen the strangest turns of fortune, the most wonderful elevations to power, the most terrible visitations of disgrace. They had seen the mightiest ruined, the brightest and most admired brought down to shame and death, men struck down with all the forms of law, whom the age honoured as its noblest ornaments. They had seen the flames of martyr or heretic, heads which had worn a crown laid one after another on the block, controversies, not merely between rivals for power, but between the deepest principles and the most rooted creeds, settled on the scaffold. Such a time of surprise,—of hope and anxiety, of horror and anguish to-day, of relief and exultation to-morrow,—had hardly been to England as the first half of the sixteenth century. All that could stir men's souls, all that could inflame their hearts, or that could wring them, had happened.

And yet, compared with previous centuries, and with what was going on abroad, the time now was a time of peace, and men lived securely. Wealth was increasing. The Wars of the Roses had left the crown powerful to enforce order, and protect industry and trade. The nation was beginning to grow rich. When the day's work was done, men's leisure was not disturbed by

the events of neighbouring war.   They had time to open
their imaginations to the great spectacle which had been
unrolled before them, to reflect upon it, to put into
shape their thoughts about it.   The intellectual movement
of the time had reached England, and its strong impulse
to mental efforts in new and untried directions was acting
powerfully upon Englishmen.   But though there was
order and present peace at home, there was much to keep
men's minds on the stretch.   There was quite enough danger and uncertainty to wind up their feelings to a high
pitch.   But danger was not so pressing as to prevent them
from giving full place to the impressions of the strange
and eventful scene round them, with its grandeur, its sadness, its promises.   In such a state of things there is
everything to tempt poetry.   There are its materials
and its stimulus, and there is the leisure to use its
materials.

But the poet had not yet been found; and everything
connected with poetry was in the disorder of ignorance
and uncertainty.   Between the counsels of a pedantic
scholarship, and the rude and hesitating, but true instincts
of the natural English ear, every one was at sea.   Yet it
seemed as if every one was trying his hand at verse.
Popular writing took that shape.   The curious and unique
record of literature preserved in the registers of the
Stationers' Company, shows that the greater proportion
of what was published, or at least entered for publication,
was in the shape of ballads.   The ballad vied with the
sermon in doing what the modern newspaper does, in
satisfying the public craving for information, amusement,
or guidance.   It related the last great novelty, the last
great battle or crime, a storm or monstrous birth.   It told
some pathetic or burlesque story, or it moralized on the

humours or follies of classes and professions, of young
and old, of men and of women. It sang the lover's hopes
or sorrows, or the adventures of some hero of history or
romance. It might be a fable, a satire, a libel, a squib,
a sacred song or paraphrase, a homily. But about all
that it treated it sought to throw more or less the colour
of imagination. It appealed to the reader's feelings, or
sympathy, or passion. It attempted to raise its subject
above the level of mere matter of fact. It sought for
choice and expressive words; it called in the help of
measure and rhythm. It aimed at a rude form of art.
Presently the critical faculty came into play. Scholars,
acquainted with classical models and classical rules, began
to exercise their judgment on their own poetry, to con-
struct theories, to review the performances before them,
to suggest plans for the improvement of the poetic art.
Their essays are curious, as the beginnings of that great
critical literature, which in England, in spite of much
infelicity, has only been second to the poetry which it
judged. But in themselves they are crude, meagre, and
helpless; interesting mainly, as showing how much craving
there was for poetry, and how little good poetry to satisfy
it, and what inconceivable doggrel could be recommended
by reasonable men, as fit to be admired and imitated.
There is fire and eloquence in Philip Sidney's *Apologie
for Poetrie* (1581); but his ideas about poetry were float-
ing, loose, and ill defined, and he had not much to point
to as of first-rate excellence in recent writers. Webbe's
Discourse of English Poetrie (1586), and the more elaborate work ascribed to George Puttenham (1589), works
of tame and artificial learning without Sidney's fire, reveal
equally the poverty, as a whole, of what had been as
yet produced in England as poetry, in spite of the wide-

D

spread passion for poetry. The specimens which they
quote and praise are mostly grotesque to the last degree.
Webbe improves some gracefully flowing lines of Spenser's into the most portentous Sapphics ; and Puttenham
squeezes compositions into the shapes of triangles, eggs,
and pilasters. Gabriel Harvey is accused by his tor-
mentor, Nash, of doing the same, " of having writ verse
in all kinds, as in form of a pair of gloves, a dozen of
points, a pair of spectacles, a two-hand sword, a poynado,
a colossus, a pyramid, a painter's easel, a market cross, a
trumpet, an anchor, a pair of pot-hooks." Puttenham's
Art of Poetry, with its books, one on Proportion, the other
on Ornament, might be compared to an Art of War, of
which one book treated of barrack drill, and the other of
busbies, sabretasches, and different forms of epaulettes and
feathers. These writers do not want good sense or the
power to make a good remark. But the stuff and material for good criticism, the strong and deep poetry, which
makes such criticisms as theirs seem so absurd, had not
yet appeared.

A change was at hand ; and the suddenness of
it is one of the most astonishing things in literary
history. The ten years from 1580 to 1590 present a set
of critical essays, giving a picture of English poetry
of which, though there are gleams of a better hope, and
praise is specially bestowed on a "new poet," the general
character is feebleness, fantastic absurdity, affectation and
bad taste. Force, and passion, and simple truth, and
powerful thoughts of the world and man, are rare ; and
poetical reformers appear maundering about miserable
attempts at English hexameters and sapphics. What
was to be looked for from all that ? Who could suppose
what was preparing under it all ? But the dawn was

come. The next ten years, from 1590 to 1600, not only
saw the *Faery Queen*, but they were the years of the
birth of the English Drama. Compare the idea which
we get of English poetry from Philip Sidney's Defense in
1581, and Puttenham's treatise in 1589, I do not say with
Shakespere, but with Lamb's selections from the Dramatic
Poets, many of them unknown names to the majority
of modern readers; and we see at once what a bound
English poetry has made; we see that a new spring time
of power and purpose in poetical thought has opened;
new and original forms have sprung to life of poetical
grandeur, seriousness, and magnificence. From the poor
and rude play-houses, with their troops of actors most
of them profligate and disreputable, their coarse excite-
ments, their buffoonery, license, and taste for the monstrous and horrible,—denounced not without reason as
corruptors of public morals, preached against at Paul's
Cross, expelled the city by the Corporation, classed by
the law with rogues, vagabonds, and sturdy beggars, and
patronized by the great and unscrupulous nobles in defiance of it—there burst forth suddenly a new poetry,
which with its reality, depth, sweetness and nobleness took
the world captive. The poetical ideas and aspirations of
the Englishmen of the time had found at last adequate
interpreters, and their own national and unrivalled
expression.

And in this great movement Spenser was the harbinger
and announcing sign. But he was only the harbinger.
What he did was to reveal to English ears as it never had
been revealed before, at least, since the days of Chaucer,
the sweet music, the refined grace, the inexhaustible versa-
tility of the English tongue. But his own efforts were in a
different direction from that profound and insatiable seek-

ing after the real, in thought and character, in representation and expression, which made Shakespere so great, and
his brethren great in proportion as they approached him.
Spenser's genius continued to the end under the influences
which were so powerful when it first unfolded itself. To
the last it allied itself, in form, at least, with the artificial.
To the last it moved in a world which was not real, which
never had existed, which, any how, was only a world of
memory and sentiment. He never threw himself frankly
on human life as it is; he always viewed it through a veil
of mist which greatly altered its true colours, and often
distorted its proportions. And thus while more than any
one he prepared the instruments and the path for the
great triumph, he himself missed the true field for the
highest exercise of poetic power; he missed the highest
honours of that in which he led the way.

Yet, curiously enough, it seems as if, early in his
career, he was affected by the strong stream which
drew Shakespere. Among the compositions of his first
period, besides *The Shepherd's Calendar*, are *Nine
Comedies*,—clearly real plays, which his friend Gabriel
Harvey praised with enthusiasm. As early as 1579
Spenser had laid before Gabriel Harvey for his judgement and advice, a portion of the *Fairy Queen* in some
shape or another, and these nine comedies. He was
standing at the parting of the ways. The allegory, with
all its tempting associations and machinery, with its
ingenuities and pictures, and boundless license to vague-
ness and to fancy, was on one side; and on the other, the
drama, with its *prima facie* and superficially prosaic
aspects, and its kinship to what was customary and
commonplace and unromantic in human life. Of the
nine comedies, composed on the model of those of Ariosto

and Machiavelli and other Italians, every trace has
perished. But this was Gabriel Harvey's opinion of the
respective value of the two specimens of work submitted
to him, and this was his counsel to their author. In April,
1580, he thus writes to Spenser.

In good faith I had once again nigh forgotten your *Faerie
Queene ;* howbeit, by good chance, I have now sent her home at
the last neither in better or worse case than I found her. And
must you of necessity have my judgement of her indeed? To
be plain, I am void of all judgement, if your *Nine Comedies,*
whereunto in imitation of Herodotus, you give the names of the
Nine Muses (and in one man's fancy not unworthily), come not
nearer Ariosto's comedies, either for the fineness of plausible
elocution, or the rareness of poetical invention, than that *Elvish
Queen* doth to his *Orlando Furioso,* which notwithstanding
you will needs seem to emulate, and hope to overgo, as you
flatly professed yourself in one of your last letters.

Besides that you know, it hath been the usual practice of the
most 'exquisite and odd wits in all nations, and specially in Italy
rather to show, and advance themselves that way than any
other : as, namely, those three notorious discoursing heads,
Bibiena, Machiavel, and Aretino did (to let Bembo and Ariosto
pass) with the great admiration and wonderment of the whole
country : being indeed reputed matchable in all points, both for
conceit of wit and eloquent deciphering of matters, either with
Aristophanes and Menander in Greek, or with Plautus and
Terence in Latin, or with any other in any other tongue.
But I will not stand greatly with you in your own matters.
If so be the *Faery Queene* be fairer in your eye than the Nine
Muses, and Hobgoblin run away with the garland from Apollo :
mark what I say, and yet I will not say that I thought, but
there is an end for this once, and fare you well, till God or some
good angel put you in a better mind.

It is plain on which side Spenser's own judgement
inclined. He had probably written the comedies, as he
had written English hexameters, out of deference to

others, or to try his hand. But the current of his own
secret thoughts, those thoughts, with their ideals and aims,
which tell a man what he is made for, and where his
power lies, set another way. The *Fairy Queen was* 'fairer
in his eye than the Nine.Muses, and Hobgoblin did run
away with the garland from Apollo.' What Gabriel Harvey
prayed for as the 'better mind' did not come. And we
cannot repine at a decision which gave us, in the shape
which it took at last, the allegory of the *Fairy Queen*.

But the *Fairy Queen*, though already planned and
perhaps begun, belongs to the last ten years of the century,
to the season of fulfilment not of promise, to the blossom-
ing, not to the opening bud. The new hopes for poetry
which Spenser brought were given in a work, which the
Fairy Queen has eclipsed and almost obscured, as the sun
puts out the morning star. Yet that which marked a
turning-point in the history of our poetry, was the book
which came out, timidly and anonymously, in the end of
1579, or the beginning of 1580, under the borrowed title
of the *Shepherd's Calendar*, a name familiar in those days
as that of an early medley of astrology and homely receipts
from time to time reprinted, which was the Moore's or
Zadkiel's almanac of the time. It was not published
ostensibly by Spenser himself, though it is inscribed to
Philip Sidney in a copy of verses signed with Spenser's
masking name of *Immerito*. The avowed responsibility
for it might have been inconvenient for a young man push-
ing his fortune among the cross currents of Elizabeth's
court. But it was given to the world by a friend of the
author's, signing himself E. K., now identified with
Spenser's fellow-student at Pembroke, Edward Kirke, who
dedicates it in a long, critical epistle of some interest to
the author's friend, Gabriel Harvey, and after the fashion

of some of the Italian books of poetry, accompanies it with
a gloss, explaining words, and to a certain extent,
allusions. Two things are remarkable in Kirke's epistle.
One is the confidence with which he announces the yet
unrecognized excellence of "this one new poet," whom he
is not afraid to put side by side with "that good old poet,"
Chaucer, the "loadstar of our language." The other point
is the absolute reliance which he places on the powers of
the English language, handled by one who has discerned
its genius, and is not afraid to use its wealth. "In my
opinion, it is one praise of many, that are due to this poet,
that he hath laboured to restore, as to their rightful
heritage, such good and natural English words, as have
been long time out of use, or almost clean disherited,
which is the only cause, that our mother tongue, which
truly of itself is both full enough for prose, and stately
enough for verse, hath long time been counted most bare
and barren of both." The friends, Kirke and Harvey,
were not wrong in their estimate of the importance of
Spenser's work. The "new poet," as he came to be
customarily called, had really made one of those distinct
steps in his art, which answer to discoveries and inven-
tions in other spheres of human interest—steps which
make all behind them seem obsolete and mistaken. There
was much in the new poetry which was immature and
imperfect, not a little that was fantastic and affected.
But it was the first adequate effort of reviving English
poetry.

The *Shepherd's Calendar* consists of twelve compositions, with no other internal connexion than that they are
assigned respectively to the twelve months of the year.
They are all different in subject, metre, character, and
excellence. They are called *Æglogues*, according to the

whimsical derivation adopted from the Italians of the
word which the classical writers called Eclogues: "*Æglogai*,
as it were αἰγῶν or αἰγονόμων λόγοι, that is, Goatherd's
Tales." The book is in its form an imitation of that
highly artificial kind of poetry which the later Italians of
the Renaissance had copied from Virgil, as Virgil had
copied it from the Sicilian and Alexandrian Greeks, and
to which had been given the name of Bucolic or Pastoral.
Petrarch, in imitation of Virgil, had written Latin Bucolics,
as he had written a Latin Epic, his *Africa*. He was followed
in the next century by Baptista Mantuanus (1448—1516),
the "old Mantuan," of Holofernes in *Love's Labour's Lost*,
whose Latin "Eglogues" became a favourite school-book
in England, and who was imitated by a writer who passed
for a poet in the time of Henry VIII., Alexander Barclay.
In the hands of the Sicilians, pastoral poetry may have
been an attempt at idealizing country life almost as genuine as some of Wordsworth's poems ; but it soon ceased
to be that, and in Alexandrian hands it took its place
among the recognized departments of classic and literary
copying, in which Virgil found and used it.   But a further
step had been made since Virgil had adopted it as an instrument of his genius.   In the hands of Mantuan and
Barclay it was a vehicle for general moralizing, and in
particular for severe satire on women and the clergy.
And Virgil, though he may himself speak under the
the names of Tityrus and Menalcas, and lament Julius
Cæsar as Daphnis, did not conceive of the Roman world
as peopled by flocks and sheep-cotes, or its emperors and
chiefs, its poets, senators, and ladies, as shepherds and
shepherdesses, of higher or lower degree.   But in Spenser's
time, partly through undue deference to what was supposed to be Italian taste, partly owing to the tardi-

ness of national culture, and because the poetic impulses
had not yet gained power to force their way through
the embarrassment and awkwardness which accompany
reviving art,—the world was turned for the purposes of
the poetry of civil life, into a pastoral scene. Poetical invention was held to consist in imagining an environment, a
set of outward circumstances, as unlike as possible to the
familiar realities of actual life and employment, in which
the primary affections and passions had their play. A
fantastic basis, varying according to the conventions of the
fashion, was held essential for the representation of the
ideal. Masquerade and hyperbole were the stage and
scenery on which the poet's sweetnesss, or tenderness, or
strength was to be put forth. The masquerade, when
his subject belonged to peace, was one of shepherds:
when it was one of war and adventure, it was a masquerade of knight errantry. But a masquerade was necessary, if he was to raise his composition above the vul-
garities and trivialities of the street, the fire-side, the camp,
or even the court; if he was to give it the dignity, the
ornament, the unexpected results, the brightness, and
colour, which belong to poetry. The fashion had the sanc-
tion of the brilliant author of the *Arcadia*, the "Courtier,
Soldier, Scholar," who was the " mould of form," and
whose judgment was law to all men of letters in the
middle years of Elizabeth, the all-accomplished Philip
Sidney. Spenser submitted to this fashion from first to
last. When first he ventured on a considerable poetical
enterprise, he spoke his thoughts, not in his own name,
nor as his contemporaries ten years later did, through the
mouth of characters in a tragic or comic drama, but
through imaginary rustics, to whom every one else in the
world was a rustic, and lived among the sheep-folds, with

a background of downs or vales or fields, and the open sky above. His shepherds and goatherds bear the homely names of native English clowns, Diggon Davie, Willye, and Piers ; Colin Clout, adopted from Skelton, stands for Spenser himself; Hobbinol, for Gabriel Harvey ; Cuddie, perhaps for Edward Kirke ; names revived by Ambrose Phillips, and laughed at by Pope, when pastorals again came into vogue with the wits of Queen Anne.[1] With them are mingled classical ones like Menalcas, French ones from Marot, anagrams like Algrind for Grindal, significant ones like Palinode, plain ones like Lettice, and romantic ones like Rosalind ; and no incongruity seems to be found in matching a beautiful shepherdess named Dido with a Great Shepherd called Lobbin, or when the verse requires it, Lobb. And not merely the speakers in the dialogue are shepherds ; every one is in their view a shepherd. Chaucer is the "god of shepherds," and Orpheus is a—

> Shepherd that did fetch his dame
> From Plutoe's baleful bower withouten leave."

The "fair Elisa," is the Queen of shepherds all ; her great father is Pan, the shepherds' god, and Anne Boleyn is Syrinx. It is not unnatural that when the clergy are spoken of, as they are in three of the poems, the figure should be kept up. But it is curious to find that the shepherd's god, the great Pan, who stands in one connexion for Henry VIII., should in another represent in sober earnest the Redeemer and Judge of the world.[2]

The poems framed in this grotesque setting, are on many themes, and of various merit, and probably of different

[1] In the *Guardian*, No. 40. Compare Johnson's *Life of Ambrose Phillips.*

[2] *Shepherd's Calendar*, May, July, and September.

dates. Some are simply amatory effusions of an ordinary
character, full of a lover's despair and complaint. Three
or four are translations or imitations; translations from
Marot, imitations from Theocritus, Bion, or Virgil. Two
of them contain fables told with great force and humour.
The story of the Oak and the Briar, related as his
friendly commentator, Kirke, says, "so lively and so
feelingly, as if the thing were set forth in some picture
before our eyes," for the warning of "disdainful
younkers," is a first fruit, and promise of Spenser's skill
in vivid narrative. The fable of the Fox and the Kid,
a curious illustration of the popular discontent at the
negligence of the clergy, and the popular suspicions about
the arts of Roman intriguers, is told with great spirit, and
with mingled humour and pathos. There is of course a
poem in honour of the great queen, who was the goddess
of their idolatry to all the wits and all the learned of
England, the "faire Eliza," and a compliment is paid to
Leicester,

> The worthy whom she loveth best,—
> That first the White Bear to the stake did bring.

Two of them are avowedly burlesque imitations of
rustic dialect and banter, carried on with much spirit.
One composition is a funeral tribute to some unknown
lady; another is a complaint of the neglect of poets by
the great. In three of the Æglogues he comes on a
more serious theme; they are vigorous satires on the loose
living and greediness of clergy forgetful of their charge,
with strong invectives against foreign corruption and
against the wiles of the wolves and foxes of Rome, with
frequent allusions to passing incidents in the guerilla war
with the seminary priests, and with a warm eulogy on
the faithfulness and wisdom of Archbishop Grindal;

whose name is disguised as old Algrind, and with whom
in his disgrace the poet is not afraid to confess deep
sympathy. They are, in a poetical form, part of that
manifold and varied system of Puritan aggression on the
established ecclesiastical order of England, which went
through the whole scale from the " Admonition to Parliament," and the lectures of Cartwright and Travers, to the
libels of Martin Mar-prelate : a system of attack which
with all its injustice and violence, and with all its mischievous purposes, found but too much justification in the
inefficiency and corruption of many both of the bishops
and clergy, and in the rapacious and selfish policy of the
government, forced to starve and cripple the public service,
while great men and favourites built up their fortunes
out of the prodigal indulgence of the Queen.

The collection of poems is thus a very miscellaneous
one, and cannot be said to be in its subjects inviting.
The poet's system of composition, also, has the disadvantage of being to a great degree unreal, forced and
unnatural. Departing from the precedent of Virgil and
the Italians, but perhaps copying the artificial Doric
of the Alexandrians, he professes to make his language
and style suitable to the " ragged and rustical " rudeness of
the shepherds whom he brings on the scene, by making
it both archaic and provincial. He found in Chaucer a
store of forms and words sufficiently well known to be
with a little help intelligible, and sufficiently out of
common use to give the character of antiquity to a poetry
which employed them. And from his sojourn in the
North he is said to have imported a certain number of
local peculiarities which would seem unfamiliar and harsh
in the South. His editor's apology for this use of
"ancient solemn words," as both proper and as orna-

mental, is worth quoting; it is an early instance of what is supposed to be not yet common, a sense of pleasure in that wildness which we call picturesque.

And first for the words to speak : I grant they be something hard, and of most men unused : yet English, and also used of most excellent Authors and most famous Poets. In whom, when as this our Poet hath been much travelled and throughly read, how could it be, (as that worthy Orator said,) but that ' walking in the sun, although for other cause he walked, yet needs he mought be sun-burnt ; and having the sound of those ancient poets still ringing in his ears, he mought needs, in singing, hit out some of their tunes. But whether he useth them by such casualty and custom, or of set purpose and choice, as thinking them fittest for such rustical rudeness of shepherds, either for that their rough sound would make his rymes more ragged and rustical, or else because such old and obsolete words are most used of country folks, sure I think, and I think not amiss, that they bring great grace, and, as one would say, authority, to the verse. . . . . Yet neither everywhere must old words be stuffed in, nor the common Dialect and manner of speaking so corrupted thereby, that, as in old buildings, it seem disorderly and ruinous. But as in most exquisite pictures they use to blaze and portrait not only the dainty lineaments of beauty, but also round about it to shadow the rude thickets and craggy cliffs, that by the baseness of such parts, more excellency may accrue to the principal—for ofttimes, we find ourselves I know not how, singularly delighted with the show of such natural rudeness, and take great pleasure in that disorderly order :—even so do these rough and harsh terms enlumine, and make more clearly to appear, the brightness of brave and glorious words. So often-times a discord in music maketh a comely concordance.

But when allowance is made for an eclectic and sometimes pedantic phraseology, and for mannerisms to which the fashion of the age tempted him, such as the extravagant use of alliteration, or, as they called it, "hunting the letter," the *Shepherd's Calendar* is, for its time, of great interest.

Spenser's force, and sustained poetical power, and singularly musical ear are conspicuous in this first essay of his genius. In the poets before him of this century, fragments and stanzas, and perhaps single pieces might be found, which might be compared with his work. Fugitive pieces, chiefly amatory, meet us of real sprightliness, or grace, or tenderness. The stanzas which Sackville, afterwards, Lord Buckhurst, contributed to the collection called the *Mirror of Magistrates*,[3] are marked with a pathetic majesty, a genuine sympathy for the precariousness of greatness, which seem a prelude to the Elizabethan drama. But these fragments were mostly felicitous efforts, which soon passed on into the ungainly, the uncouth, the obscure or the grotesque. But in the *Shepherd's Calendar* we have for the first time in the century, the swing, the command, the varied resources of the real poet, who is not driven by failing language or thought into frigid or tumid absurdities. Spenser is master over himself and his instrument even when he uses it in a way which offends our taste. There are passages in the *Shepherd's Calendar* of poetical eloquence, of refined vigour, and of musical and imaginative sweetness, such as the English language had never attained to, since the days of him, who was to the age of Spenser, what Shakespere and Milton are to ours, the pattern and fount of poetry, Chaucer. Dryden is not afraid to class Spenser with Theocritus and Virgil, and to write that the *Shepherd's Calendar* is not to be matched in any language.[4] And this was at once recognized. The authorship of it, as has been said, was not formally acknowledged. In-

[3] First published in 1559. It was popular book, and was often re-edited.
[4] Dedication to Virgil.

deed, Mr. Collier remarks that seven years after its publication, and after it had gone through three or four separate editions, it was praised by a contemporary poet, George Whetstone, himself a friend of Spenser's, as the "reputed work of Sir. Philip Sidney." But if it was officially a secret, it was an open secret, known to every one who cared to be well informed. It is possible that the free language used in it about ecclesiastical abuses was too much in sympathy with the growing fierceness and insolence of Puritan invective to be safely used by a poet who gave his name : and one of the reasons assigned for Burghley's dislike to Spenser is the praise bestowed in the *Shepherd's Calendar* on Archbishop Grindal, then in deep disgrace for resisting the suppression of the puritan prophesyings. But anonymous as it was, it had been placed under Sidney's protection ; and it was at once warmly welcomed. It is not often that in those remote days we get evidence of the immediate effect of a book ; but we have this evidence in Spenser's case. In this year, probably, after it was published, we find it spoken of by Philip Sidney, not without discriminating criticism, but as one of the few recent examples of poetry worthy to be named after Chaucer.

I account the *Mirror of Magistrates* meetly furnished of beautiful parts ; and in the Earl of Surrey's *Lyrics* many things tasting of birth, and worthy of a noble mind. The *Shepherd's Calendar* hath much poetry in his Eglogues : indeed worthy the reading if I be not deceived. That same framing of his style in an old rustic language I dare not allow, sith neither Theocritus in Greek, Virgil in Latin, nor Sanazar in Italian, did affect it. Besides these do I not remember to have seen but few (to speak boldly) printed that have poetical sinews in them.

Sidney's patronage of the writer and general approval

of the work doubtless had something to do with making
Spenser's name known : but he at once takes a place in
contemporary judgment which no one else takes, till the
next decade of the century. In 1586, Webbe published
his *Discouse of English Poetrie.* In this, the author
of the *Shepherd's Calendar* is spoken of by the name
given him by its Editor, E. K——, as the " new poet,"
just as earlier in the century, the *Orlando Furioso* was
styled the "nuova poesia ;" and his work is copiously
used to supply examples and illustrations of the critic's
rules and observations. Webbe's review of existing poetry
was the most comprehensive yet attempted : but the
place which he gives to the new poet, whose name was
in men's mouths, though like the author of *In Memo-
riam,* he had not placed it on his title-page, was one
quite apart.

This place [to wear the Laurel] have I purposely reserved for
one, who, if not only, yet in my judgement principally, deserveth
the title of the rightest English poet that ever I read : that is,
the author of the *Shepherd's Calendar,* intituled to the worthy
Gentleman Master Philip Sidney, whether it was Master Sp. or
what rare scholar in Pembroke Hall soever, because himself and
his friends, for what respect I know not, would not reveal it,
I force not greatly to set down. Sorry I am that I cannot find
none other with whom I might couple him in this catalogue in
his rare gift of poetry : although one there is, though now long
since seriously occupied in graver studies, Master Gabriel Harvey,
yet as he was once his most special friend and fellow poet, so
because he hath taken such pains not only in his Latin poetry
. . . but also to reform our English verse. . . therefore will I
adventure to set them together as two of the rarest wits and
learnedest masters of poetry in England.

He even ventured to compare him favourably with
Virgil.

But now yet at the last hath England hatched up one poet of this sort, in my conscience comparable with the best in any respect : even Master Sp., author of the *Shepherd's Calendar*, whose travail in that piece of English poetry I think verily is so commendable, as none of equal judgement can yield him less praise for his excellent skill and skilful excellency showed forth in the same than they would to either Theocritus or Virgil, whom in mine opinion, if the coarseness of our speech, (I mean the course of custom which he would not infringe,) had been no more let unto him than their pure native tongues were unto them, he would have, if it might be, surpassed them.

The courtly author of the *Arte of English Poesie*, 1589, commonly cited as G. Puttenham, classes him with Sidney. And from this time his name occurs in every enumeration of English poetical writers, till he appears, more than justifying this early appreciation of his genius, as Chaucer's not unworthy successor, in the *Faery Queen*. Afterwards, as other successful poetry was written, and the standards of taste were multiplied, this first enthusiastic reception cooled down. In James the First's time, Spenser's use of " old outworn words " is criticized as being no more "practical English " than Chaucer or Skelton: it is not "courtly" enough.[5] The success of the *Shepherd's Calendar* had also, apparently, substantial results, which some of his friends thought of with envy. They believed that it secured him high patronage, and opened to him a way to fortune. Poor Gabriel Harvey, writing in the year in which the *Shepherd's Calendar* came out, contrasts his own less favoured lot, and his ill-repaid poetical efforts, with Colin Clout's good luck.

But ever and ever, methinks, your great Catoes, *Ecquid erit pretii*, and our little Catoes, *Res age quæ prosunt*, make such

---

[5] Bolton in Haslewood, ii. 249.

E

a buzzing and ringing in my head, that I have little joy to
animate and encourage either you or him to go forward, unless
ye might make account of some certain ordinary wages, or at the
least wise have your meat and drink for your day's works. As
for myself, howsoever I have toyed and trifled heretofore, I am
now taught, and I trust I shall shortly learn, (no remedy, I must
of mere necessity give you over in the plain field) to employ my
travail and time wholly or chiefly on those studies and practices
that carry, as they say, meat in their mouth, having evermore
their eye upon the Title, *De pane lucrando,* and their hand
upon their halfpenny. For I pray now what saith Mr. Cuddie,
alias you know who, in the tenth Æglogue of the aforesaid
famous new Calendar.

*   *   *   *   *

> The dapper ditties, that I wont devise
> To feed youths' fancy and the flocking fry,
> Delighten much : what I the best for thy ?
> They han the pleasure, I a sclender prize.
> I beat the bush, the birds to them do fly.
> What good thereof to Cuddie can arise ?

But Master Colin Clout is not everybody, and albeit his old
companions, Master Cuddie and Master Hobinoll, be as little
beholding to their mistress poetry as ever you wist: yet he,
peradventure, by the means of her special favour, and some
personal privilege, may haply live by *Dying Pelicans,* and pur-
chase great lands and lordships with 'the money which his
Calendar and *Dreams* have, and will afford him.

CHAPTER III.

[1580.]

IN the first week of October, 1579, Spenser was at Leicester House, expecting "next week" to be despatched on Leicester's service to France. Whether he was sent or not, we do not know. Gabriel Harvey, writing at the end of the month, wagers that "for all his saying, he will not be gone over sea, neither this week nor the next." In one of the Æglogues (September) there are some lines which suggest, but do not necessarily imply, the experience of an eye-witness of the state of religion in a Roman Catholic country. But we can have nothing but conjecture whether at this time or any other Spenser was on the Continent. The *Shepherd's Calendar* was entered at Stationers' Hall, December 5, 1579. In April, 1580, as we know from one of his letters to Harvey, he was at Westminster. He speaks of the *Shepherd's Calendar* as published; he is contemplating the publication of other pieces, and then "he will in hand forthwith with his *Fairie Queene*," of which he had sent Harvey a specimen. He speaks especially of his *Dreams* as a considerable work.

I take best my *Dreams* should come forth alone, being grown

by means of the Gloss (running continually in manner of a
Paraphrase) full as great as my *Calendar*. Therein be some
things excellently, and many things wittily discoursed of E. K.,
and the pictures so singularly set forth and portrayed, as if
Michael Angelo were there, he could (I think) nor amend the
best, nor reprehend the worst. I know you would like them
passing well.

It is remarkable that of a book so spoken of, as of the
Nine Comedies, not a trace, as far as appears, is to be
found. He goes on to speak with much satisfaction of
another composition, which was probably incorporated,
like the *Epithalamion Thamesis*, in his later work.

Of my *Stemmata Dudleiana*, and specially of the sundry
Apostrophes therein, addressed you know to whom, much more
advisement he had, than so lightly to send them abroad : now
list, trust me (though I do never very well) yet, in mine own
fancy, I never did better. *Veruntamen te sequor solum : nunquam vero assequar.*

He is plainly not dissatisfied with his success, and is
looking forward to more. But no one in those days could
live by poetry. Even scholars, in spite of university en-
dowments, did not hope to live by their scholarship ; and
the poet or man of letters only trusted that his work, by
attracting the favour of the great, might open to him the
door of advancement. Spenser was probably expecting
to push his fortunes in some public employment under
the patronage of two such powerful favourites as Sidney
and his uncle Leicester. Spenser's heart was set on
poetry : but what leisure he might have for it would
depend on the course his life might take. To have hung
on Sidney's protection, or gone with him as his secretary
to the wars, to have been employed at home or abroad
in Leicester's intrigues, to have stayed in London filling

by Leicester's favour some government office, to have
had his habits moulded and his thoughts affected by
the brilliant and unscrupulous society of the court, or by
the powerful and daring minds which were fast thronging
the political and literary scene—any of these contingencies
might have given his poetical faculty a different direction;
nay, might have even abridged its exercise or suppressed
it. But his life was otherwise ordered. A new opening
presented itself. He had, and he accepted, the chance
of making his fortune another way. And to his new
manner of life, with its peculiar conditions, may be ascribed, not indeed the original idea of that which was to
be his great work, but the circumstances under which
the work was carried out, and which not merely coloured
it, but gave it some of its special and characteristic
features.

That which turned the course of his career, and exercised
a decisive influence, certainly on its events and fate, probably also on the turn of his thoughts and the shape and
moulding of his work, was his migration to Ireland, and his
settlement there for the greater part of the remaining
eighteen years of his life. We know little more than the
main facts of this change from the court and the growing
intellectual activity of England, to the fierce and narrow
interests of a cruel and unsuccessful struggle for coloniza-
tion, in a country which was to England much what
Algeria was to France some thirty years ago. Ireland,
always unquiet, had became a serious danger to Elizabeth's
Government. It was its "bleeding ulcer." Lord Essex's
great colonizing scheme, with his unscrupulous severity,
had failed. Sir Henry Sidney, wise, firm, and wishing
to be just, had tried his hand as Deputy for the third time
in the thankless charge of keeping order; he, too, after a

short gleam of peace, had failed also. For two years Ireland
had been left to the local administration, totally unable to
heal its wounds, or cope with its disorders. And now,
the kingdom threatened to become a vantage-ground to the
foreign enemy. In November, 1579, the Government
turned their eyes on Arthur, Lord Grey of Wilton, a man
of high character, and a soldier of distinction. He, or
they, seem to have hesitated ; or rather, the hesitation was
on both sides. He was not satisfied with many things in
the policy of the Queen in England : his discontent had
led him, strong Protestant as he was, to coquet with Norfolk and the partisans of Mary Queen of Scots, when
England was threatened with a French marriage ten years
before. His name stands among the forty nobles on
whom Mary's friends counted.[1] And on the other hand,
Elizabeth did not like him or trust him. For some time
she refused to employ him. At length, in the summer of
1580, he was appointed to fill that great place which had
wrecked the reputation and broken the hearts of a succession of able and high-spirited servants of the English
Crown, the place of Lord-Deputy in Ireland. He was a
man who was interested in the literary enterprise of the
time. In the midst of his public employment in Holland,
he had been the friend and patron of George Gascoigne,
who left a high reputation, for those days, as poet, wit,
satirist, and critic. Lord Grey now took Spenser, the
"new poet," the friend of Philip Sidney, to Ireland as his
Secretary.

Spenser was not the only scholar and poet who about
this time found public employment in Ireland. Names
which appear in literary records, such as Warton's *History
of English Poetry*, poets like Barnaby Googe and Ludovic

[1] Froude, x. 158.

Bryskett, reappear as despatch-writers or agents in the
Irish State Papers. But one man came over to Ireland
about the same time as Spenser, whose fortunes were a
contrast to his. Geoffrey Fenton was one of the numerous translators of the time. He had dedicated Tragical
Tales from the French and Italian to Lady Mary Sidney,
Guevara's Epistles from the Spanish to Lady Oxford, and
a translation of Guicciardini to the Queen. About this
time, he was recommended by his brother to Walsingham for foreign service; he was soon after in Ireland:
and in the summer of 1580, he was made Secretary to
the Government. He shortly became one of the most
important persons in the Irish administration. He corresponded confidentially and continually with Burghley
and Walsingham. He had his eye on the proceedings
of Deputies and Presidents, and reported freely their
misdoings or their unpopularity. His letters form a
considerable part of the Irish Papers. He became a
powerful and successful public servant. He became Sir
Geoffrey Fenton; he kept his high place for his life; he
obtained grants and lands; and he was commemorated
as a great personage, in a pompous monument in St.
Patrick's Cathedral. This kind of success was not to be
Spenser's.

Lord Grey of Wilton was a man in whom his friends
saw a high and heroic spirit. He was a statesman in
whose motives and actions his religion had a dominant
influence : and his religion—he is called by the vague
name of Puritan—was one which combined a strong and
doubtless genuine zeal for the truth of Christian doctrine
and for purity of morals, with the deepest and deadliest
hatred of what he held to be their natural enemy, the
Anti-Christ of Rome. The "good Lord Grey," he was, if

we believe his secretary, writing many years after this
time, and when he was dead, " most gentle, affable, loving,
and temperate ; always known to be a most just, sincere,
godly, and right noble man, far from sternness, far from
unrighteousness." But the infelicity of his times bore
hardly upon him, and Spenser admits, what is known
otherwise, that he left a terrible name behind him. He
was certainly a man of severe and unshrinking sense of
duty, and like many great Englishmen of the time, so
resolute in carrying it out to the end, that it reached,
when he thought it necessary, to the point of ferocity. Naturally, he had enemies, who did not spare his fame ; and
Spenser, who came to admire and reverence him, had to
lament deeply that "that good lord was blotted with the
name of a bloody man," one who " regarded not the life
of the queen's subjects no more than dogs, and had wasted
and consumed all, so as now she had nothing almost left,
but to reign in their ashes."

Lord Grey was sent over at a moment of the utmost
confusion and danger. In July, 1579, Drury wrote to
Burghley to stand firmly to the helm, for "that a great
storm was at hand." The South of Ireland was in fierce
rebellion, under the Earl of Desmond and Dr. Nicolas
Sanders, who was acting under the commission of the
Pope, and promising the assistance of the King of Spain ;
and a band of Spanish and Italian adventurers, unautho-
rized, but not uncountenanced by their Government, like
Drake in the Indies, had landed with arms and stores, and
had fortified a port at Smerwick, on the south-western
coast of Kerry. The North was deep in treason, restless,
and threatening to strike. Round Dublin itself, the great
Irish Lords of the Pale, under Lord Baltinglass, in the
summer of 1580, had broken into open insurrection, and

were holding out a hand to the rebels of the South. The
English garrisons, indeed, small as they were, could not
only hold their own against the ill-armed and undis-
ciplined Irish bands, but could inflict terrible chastisement
on the insurgents. The native feuds were turned to account ; Butlers were set to destroy their natural enemies
the Geraldines, and the Earl of Ormond their head,
was appointed General in Munster, to execute English
vengeance and his own on the lands and people of his
rival Desmond. But the English chiefs were not strong
enough to put down the revolt. "The conspiracy throughout Ireland," wrote Lord Grey, "is so general, that without a main force it will not be appeased. There are cold
service and unsound dealing generally." On the 12th
of August, 1580, Lord Grey landed, amid a universal
wreck of order, of law, of mercy, of industry ; and among
his counsellors and subordinates, the only remedy thought
of was that of remorseless and increasing severity.

It can hardly be doubted that Spenser must have come
over with him. It is likely that where he went, his
Secretary would accompany him. And if so, Spenser
must soon have become acquainted with some of the
scenes and necessities of Irish life. Within three weeks
after Lord Grey's landing, he and those with him were
present at the disaster of Glenmalure, a rocky defile near
Wicklow, where the rebels enticed the English captains
into a position in which an ambuscade had been prepared,
after the manner of Red Indians in the last century, and
of South African savages now, and where, in spite of Lord
Grey's courage, "which could not have been bettered by
Hercules," a bloody defeat was inflicted on his troops, and
a number of distinguished officers were cut off. But
Spenser was soon to see a still more terrible example of

this ruthless warfare.   It was necessary, above all things
to destroy the Spanish fort at Smerwick, in order to prevent the rebellion being fed from abroad : and in November, 1580, Lord Grey in person undertook the work.   The
incidents of this tragedy have been fully recorded, and
they formed at the time a heavy charge against Lord
Grey's humanity, and even his honour.   In this instance
Spenser must almost certainly have been on the spot.
Years afterwards, in his *View of the State of Ireland,* he
describes and vindicates Lord Grey's proceedings ; and he
does so, " being," as he writes, " as near them as any."
And we have Lord Grey's own despatch to Queen Elizabeth, containing a full report of the tragical business.
We have no means of knowing how Lord Grey employed
Spenser, or whether he composed his own despatches.
But from Spenser's position, the Secretary, if he had not
some hand in the following vivid and forcible account of
the taking of Smerwick,[2] must probably have been cogni-
zant of it ; though there are some slight differences in
the despatch, and in the account which Spenser himself
wrote afterwards in his pamphlet on Irish Affairs.

After describing the proposal of the garrison for a
parley, Lord Grey proceeds,—

There was presently sent unto me one Alexandro, their camp
master; he told me that certain Spaniards and Italians were
there arrived upon fair speeches and great promises, which
altogether vain and false they found ; and that it was no part
of their intent to molest or take any government from your
Majesty ; for proof, that they were ready to depart as they
came and deliver into my hands the fort.   Mine answer was,
that for that I perceived their people to stand of two nations,

<hr>

[2] Calendar of State Papers Ireland, 1574—1585. Mr. H. C.
Hamilton's Pref. p. lxxi—lxxiii. Nov. 12, 1580.

Italian and Spanish, I would give no answer unless a Spaniard
was likewise by. He presently went and returned with a
Spanish captain. I then told the Spaniard that I knew their
nation to have an absolute prince, one that was in good league
and amity with your Majesty, which made me to marvell that
any of his people should be found associate with them that went
about to maintain rebels against you. . . And taking it that it
could not be his king's will, I was to know by whom and for
what cause they were sent. His reply was that the king had
not sent them, but that one John Martinez de Ricaldi, Governor
for the king at Bilboa, had willed him to levy a band and repair
with it to St. Andrews (Santander), and there to be directed by
this their colonel here, whom he followed as a blind man, not
knowing whither. The other avouched that they were all sent
by the Pope for the defence of the *Catholica fede.* My answer
was, that I would not greatly have marvelled if men being commanded by natural and absolute princes did sometimes take in
hand wrong actions; but that men, and that of account as some
of them made show of, should be carried into unjust, desperate,
and wicked actions, by one that neither from God or man could
claim any princely power or empire, but (was) indeed a detest-
able shaveling, the right Antichrist and general ambitious
tyrant over all right principalities, and patron of the *Diabolica
fede*—this I could not but greatly rest in wonder. Their fault
therefore far to be aggravated by the vileness of their com-
mander; and that at my hands no condition or composition they
were to expect, other than they should render me the fort, and
yield their selves to my will for life or death. With this answer
he departed; after which there was one or two courses to and
fro more, to have gotten a certainty for some of their lives: but
finding that it would not be, the colonel himself about sunsetting
came forth and requested respite with surcease of arms till the
next morning, and then he would give a resolute answer.

Finding that to be but a gain of time to them, and a loss of
the same for myself, I definitely answered I would not grant
it, and therefore presently either that he took my offer or else
return and I would fall to my business. He then embraced my
knees simply putting himself to my mercy, only he prayed that

for that night he might abide in the fort, and that in the morning all should be put into my hands. I asked hostages for the
performance; they were given. Morning came; I presented
my companies in battle before the fort, the colonel comes forth
with ten or twelve of his chief gentlemen, trailing their ensigns
rolled up, and presented them unto me with their lives and the
fort. I sent straight certain gentlemen in, to see their weapons
and armour laid down, and to guard the munition and victual
there left for spoil.   Then put I in certain bands, who straight
fell to execution. There were six hundred slain. Munition and
victual great store : though much wasted through the disorder of
the soldier, which in that fury could not be helped. Those that I
gave life unto, I have bestowed upon the captains and gentlemen whose service hath well deserved. . . Of the six hundred
slain, four hundred were as gallant and goodly personages as of
any (soldiers) I ever beheld. So hath it pleased the Lord of
Hosts to deliver your enemies into your Highnesses' hand, and
so too as one only excepted, not one of yours is either lost or
hurt.

Another account adds to this that "the Irish men and
women were hanged, with an Englishman who had served
Dr. Sanders, and two others whose arms and legs were
broken for torture."

Such scenes as those of Glenmalure and Smerwick,
terrible as they were, it might have been any one's lot to
witness who found himself in presence of the atrocious
warfare of those cruel days, in which the ordinary exas-
peration of combatants was made more savage and unfor-
giving by religious hatred, and by the license which
religious hatred gave to irregular adventure and the san-
guinary repression of it. They were not confined to
Ireland. Two years later the Marquis de Santa Cruz
treated in exactly the same fashion a band of French
adventurers, some eighty noblemen and gentlemen and
two hundred soldiers, who were taken in an attempt on

the Azores during a time of nominal peace between the
crowns of France and Spain. In the Low Countries, and
in the religious wars of France, it need not be said that
even the 'execution' at Smerwick was continually out-
done; and it is what the Spaniards would of course have
done to Drake if they had caught him. Nor did the
Spanish Government complain of this treatment of its
subjects, who had no legal commission.

But the change of scene and life to Spenser was much
more than merely the sight of a disastrous skirmish and
a capitulation without quarter. He had passed to an
entirely altered condition of social life; he had passed
from pleasant and merry England, with its comparative
order and peace, its thriving homesteads and wealthy
cities, its industry and magnificence,—

Eliza's blessed field,
That still with people, peace, and plenty flows—

to a land, beautiful indeed, and alluring, but of which
the only law was disorder, and the only rule failure.
The Cambridge student, the follower of country life in
Lancashire or Kent, the scholar discussing with Philip
Sidney and corresponding with Gabriel Harvey about
classical metres and English rimes; the shepherd poet,
Colin Clout, delicately fashioning his innocent pastorals,
his love complaints, or his dexterous panegyrics or satires;
the courtier, aspiring to shine in the train of Leicester
before the eyes of the great queen,—found himself trans-
planted into a wild and turbulent savagery, where the
elements of civil society hardly existed, and which had
the fatal power of drawing into its own evil and lawless
ways the English who came into contact with it. Ireland
had the name and the framework of a Christian realm.
It had its hierarchy of officers in Church and State, its

Parliament, its representative of the Crown. It had its great earls and lords, with noble and romantic titles, its courts and councils and administration; the Queen's laws were there, and where they were acknowledged, which was not, however, everywhere, the English speech was current. But underneath this name and outside, all was coarse, and obstinately set against civilized order. There was nothing but the wreck and clashing of disintegrated customs, the lawlessness of fierce and ignorant barbarians, whose own laws had been destroyed, and who would recognize no other; the blood-feuds of rival septs; the ambitious and deadly treacheries of rival nobles, oppressing all weaker than themselves, and maintaining in waste and idleness their crowds of brutal retainers. In one thing only was there agreement, though not even in this was there union; and that was in deep, implacable hatred of their English masters. And with these English masters, too, amid their own jealousies and backbitings and mischief-making, their own bitter antipathies and chronic despair, there was only one point of agreement, and that was their deep scorn and loathing of the Irish.

This is Irish dealing with Irish, in Munster at this time :—

The Lord Roche kept a freeholder, who had eight plowlands, prisoner, and hand-locked him till he had surrendered seven plowlands and a half, on agreement to keep the remaining plowland free; but when this was done, the Lord Roche extorted as many exactions from that half-plowland, as from any other half-plowland in his country. . . . And even the great men were under the same oppression from the greater: for the Earl of Desmond forcibly took away the Seneschal of Imokilly's corn from his own land, though he was one of the most considerable gentlemen in Munster.[3]

---

[3] Cox, Hist. of Ireland, 354.

And this is English dealing with Irish :—

Mr. Henry Sheffield asks Lord Burghley's interest with Sir George Carew, to be made his deputy at Leighlin, in place of Mr. Bagenall, who met his death under the following circumstances :—

Mr. Bagenall, after he had bought the barony of Odrone of Sir George Carew, could not be contented to let the Kavanaghs enjoy such lands as old Sir Peter Carew, young Sir Peter, and last, Sir George were content that they should have, but threatened to kill them wherever he could meet them. As it is now fallen out, about the last of November, one Henry Heron, Mr. Bagenall's brother-in-law, having lost four kine, making that his quarrel, he being accompanied with divers others to the number of twenty or thereabouts, by the procurement of his brother-in-law, went to the house of Mortagh Oge, a man seventy years old, the chief of the Kavanaghs, with their swords drawn : which the old man seeing, for fear of his life, sought to go into the woods, but was taken and brought before Mr. Heron, who charged him that his son had taken the cows. The old man answered that he could pay for them. Mr. Heron would not be contented, but bade his men kill him, he desiring to be brought for trial at the sessions. Further, the morrow after they went again into the woods, and there they found another old man, a servant of Mortagh Oge, and likewise killed him, Mr. Heron saying that it was because he would not confess the cows.

On these murders, the sons of the old man laid an ambush for Mr. Bagenall; who, following them more upon will than with discretion, fell into their hands, and were slain with thirteen more. He had sixteen wounds above his girdle, and one of his legs cut off, and his tongue drawn out of his mouth and slit. There is not one man dwelling in all this country that was Sir George Carew's, but every man fled, and left the whole country waste; and so I fear me it will continue, now the deadly feud is so great between them.[4]

Something like this has been occasionally seen in our

[4] Irish Papers, March 29, 1587.

colonies towards the native races; but there it never reached
the same height of unrestrained and frankly justified indulgence. The English officials and settlers knew well enough
that the only thought of the native Irish was to restore
their abolished customs, to recover their confiscated lands,
to re-establish the crippled power of their chiefs; they
knew that for this insurrection was ever ready, and that
treachery would shrink from nothing. And to meet it,
the English on the spot—all but a few who were denounced as unpractical sentimentalists for favouring an
irreconcilable foe—could think of no way of enforcing
order, except by a wholesale use of the sword and the
gallows. They could find no means of restoring peace
except turning the rich land into a wilderness, and root-
ing out by famine those whom the soldier or the hangman
had not overtaken. "No governor shall do any good
here," wrote an English observer in 1581, "except he
show himself a Tamerlane."

In a general account, even contemporary, such statements
might suggest a violent suspicion of exaggeration. We
possess the means of testing it. The Irish State Papers of
the time contain the ample reports and letters, from day
to day, of the energetic and resolute Englishmen employed
in council or in the field—men of business like Sir
William Pelham, Sir Henry Wallop, Edward Waterhouse,
and Geoffrey Fenton;—daring and brilliant officers, like
Sir William Drury, Sir Nicolas Malby, Sir Warham St.
Leger, Sir John Norreys, and John Zouch. These papers
are the basis of Mr. Froude's terrible chapters on the Desmond rebellion, and their substance in abstract or abridg-
ment is easily accessible in the printed calendars of the
Record Office. They show that from first to last, in
principle and practice, in council and in act, the Tamer-

lane system was believed in, and carried out without a
trace of remorse or question as to its morality. "If hell
were open, and all the evil spirits were abroad," writes
Walsingham's correspondent Andrew Trollope, who talked
about Tamerlane, "they could never be worse than these
Irish rogues—rather dogs, and worse than dogs, for dogs
do but after their kind, and they degenerate from all
humanity." There is but one way of dealing with wild
dogs or wolves ; and accordingly the English chiefs insisted
that this was the way to deal with the Irish. The state
of Ireland, writes one, "is like an old cloak often before
patched, wherein is now made so great a gash that all the
world doth know that there is no remedy but to make a
new." This means, in the language of another, "that
there is no way to daunt these people but by the edge of
the sword, and to plant better in their place, or rather, let
them cut one another's throats." These were no idle
words. Every page of these papers contains some memo-
randum of execution and destruction. The progress
of a Deputy, or the President of a province, through the
country is always accompanied with its tale of hangings.
There is sometimes a touch of the grotesque. "At
Kilkenny," writes Sir W. Drury, "the jail being full, we
caused sessions immediately to begin. Thirty-six persons
were executed, among which some good ones ; two for
treason, a blackamoor, and two witches by natural law,
for that we found no law to try them by in this realm."
It is like the account of some unusual kind of game in a
successful bag. "If taking of cows, and killing of kerne
and churles had been worth advertizing," writes Lord
Grey to the Queen, "I would have had every day to have
troubled your Highness." Yet Lord Grey protests in the
same letter that he has never taken the life of any, how-

F

ever evil, who submitted. At the end of the Desmond
outbreak, the chiefs in the different provinces send in their
tale of death. Ormond complains of the false reports of
his "slackness in but killing three men," whereas the
number was more than 3000; and he sends in his "brief
note" of his contribution to the slaughter, "598 persons
of quality, besides 3000 or 4000 others, and 158 slain
since his discharge." The end was that, as one of the
chief actors writes, Sir Warham St. Leger, "Munster is
nearly unpeopled by the murders done by the rebels, and
the killings by the soldiers; 30,000 dead of famine in
half a year, besides numbers that are hanged and killed.
The realm," he adds, "was never in greater danger, or in
like misery." But in the murderous work itself there was
not much danger. "Our wars," writes Sir Henry Wallop,
in the height of the struggle, "are but like fox-hunting."
And when the English Government remonstrates against
this system of massacre, the Lord-Deputy writes back that
"he sorrows that pity for the wicked and evil should be
enchanted into her Majesty."

And of this dreadful policy, involving, as the price of
the extinction of Desmond's rebellion, the absolute desolation of the South and West of Ireland, Lord Grey came
to be the deliberate and unfaltering champion. His administration lasted only two years, and in spite of his natural
kindness of temper, which we need not doubt, it was, from
the supposed necessities of his position, and the unwaver-
ing consent of all English opinions round him, a rule of
extermination. No scruple ever crossed his mind, except
that he had not been sufficiently uncompromising in putting first the religious aspect of the quarrel. "If Elizabeth
had allowed him," writes Mr. Froude, "he would have now
made a Mahommedan conquest of the whole island, and

offered the Irish the alternative of the Gospel or the sword."
With the terrible sincerity of a Puritan, he reproached
himself that he had allowed even the Queen's commands
to come before the "one article of looking to God's dear
service." "I confess my sin," he wrote to Walsingham,
"I have followed man too much," and he saw why his
efforts had been in vain. "Baal's prophets and councillors
shall prevail. I see it is so. I see it is just. I see it past
help. I rest despaired." His policy of blood and devasta-
tion, breaking the neck of Desmond's rebellion, but failing
to put an end to it, became at length more than the home
Government could bear; and with mutual dissatisfaction
he was recalled before his work was done. Among the
documents relating to his explanations with the English
Government, is one of which this is the abstract: "De-
claration (Dec. 1583), by Arthur, Lord Grey, of Wilton, to
the Queen, showing the state of Ireland when he was appointed Deputy, with the services of his government, and
the plight he left it in. 1485 chief men and gentlemen
slain, not accounting those of meaner sort, nor yet execu-
tions by law, and killing of churles, which were innume-
rable."

This was the world into which Spenser was abruptly
thrown, and in which he was henceforward to have his
home. He first became acquainted with it as Lord Grey's
Secretary in the Munster war. He himself in later days
with ample experience and knowledge reviewed the whole
of this dreadful history, its policy, its necessities, its
results : and no more instructive document has come
down to us from those times. But his description of the
way in which the plan of extermination was carried out in
Munster before his eyes, may fittingly form a supplement
to the language on the spot of those responsible for it.

Eudox. But what, then, shall be the conclusion of this war ? . . .

Iren.—The end will I assure me be very short and much sooner than can be, in so great a trouble, as it seemeth, hoped for, although there should none of them fall by the sword nor be slain by the soldier : yet thus being kept from manurance and their cattle from running abroad, by this hard restraint they would quickly consume themselves, and devour one another. The proof whereof I saw sufficiently exampled in these late wars of Munster; for notwithstanding that the same was a most rich and plentiful country, full of corn and cattle that you would have thought they should have been able to stand long, yet ere one year and a half they were brought to such wretchedness as that any stony heart would have rued the same. Out of every corner of the woods and glynnes they came creeping forth upon their hands, for their legs could not bear them ; they looked like anatomies of death, they spake like ghosts crying out of their graves; they did eat the dead carrions, happy where they could find them, yea and one another soon after, insomuch that the very carcases they spared not to scrape out of their graves ; and if they found a plot of water-cresses or shamrocks, there they flocked as to a feast for a time, yet not able long to continue there withal ; that in a short space there were none almost left, and a most populous and plentiful country suddenly left void of man and beast ; yet sure ·in all that war there perished not many by the sword, but all by the extremity of famine which they themselves had wrought.

It is hardly surprising that Lord Grey's Secretary should share the opinions and the feelings of his master and patron. Certainly in his company and service, Spenser learned to look upon Ireland and the Irish with the impatience and loathing which filled most Englishmen ; and it must be added with the same greedy eyes. In this new atmosphere, in which his life was henceforth spent, amid the daily talk of ravage and death, the daily scramble for the spoils of rebels and traitors,

the daily alarms of treachery and insurrection, a man
naturally learns hardness. Under Spenser's imaginative
richness, and poetic delicacy of feeling, there appeared two
features. There was a shrewd sense of the practical side
of things : and there was a full share of that sternness of
temper which belonged to the time. He came to Ireland
for no romantic purpose : he came to make his fortune
as well as he could : and he accepted the conditions of
the place and scene, and entered at once, into the game
of adventure and gain which was the natural one for all
English comers, and of which the prizes were lucrative
offices and forfeited manors and abbeys. And in the
native population and native interests, he saw nothing
but what called forth not merely antipathy, but deep
moral condemnation. It was not merely that the Irish
were ignorant, thriftless, filthy, debased and loathsome in
their pitiable misery and despair: it was that in his
view, justice, truth, honesty had utterly perished among
them, and therefore were not due to them.   Of any
other side to the picture, he like other good Englishmen,
was entirely unconscious: he saw only on all sides of
him the empire of barbarism and misrule which valiant
and godly Englishmen were fighting to vanquish and
destroy—fighting against apparent but not real odds. And
all this was aggravated by the stiff adherence of the Irish
to their old religion. Spenser came over with the common opinion of Protestant Englishmen, that they had at
least in England the pure and undoubted religion of the
Bible : and in Ireland, he found himself face to face with
the very superstition in its lowest forms which he had so
hated in England. He left it plotting in England; he
found it in armed rebellion in Ireland. Like Lord Grey,
he saw in Popery the root of all the mischiefs of Ireland ;

and his sense of true religion, as well as his convictions of right, conspired to recommend to him Lord Grey's pitiless government. The opinion was everywhere—it was undisputed and unexamined—that a policy of force, direct or indirect, was the natural and right way of reducing diverging religions to submission and uniformity : that religious disagreement ought as a matter of principle to be subdued by violence of one degree or another. All wise and good men thought so : all statesmen and rulers acted so. Spenser found in Ireland a state of things which seemed to make this doctrine the simplest dictate of common sense.

In August, 1582, Lord Grey left Ireland. He had accepted his office with the utmost reluctance, from the known want of agreement between the Queen and himself as to policy. He had executed it in a way which greatly displeased the home Government. And he gave it up with his special work, the extinction of Desmond's rebellion, still unaccomplished. In spite of the thousands slain, and a province made a desert, Desmond was still at large and dangerous. Lord Grey had been ruthlessly severe, and yet not successful. For months there had been an interchange of angry letters between him and the Government. Burghley, he complains to Walsingham, was " so heavy against him." The Queen and Burghley wanted order restored, but did not like either the expense of war, or the responsibility before other governments for the severity which their agents on the spot judged necessary. Knowing that he did not please, he had begun to solicit his recall before he had been a year in Ireland ; and at length he was recalled, not to receive thanks, but to meet a strict, if not hostile, inquiry into his administration. Besides what had been on the surface

of his proceedings to dissatisfy the Queen, there had been,
as in the case of every Deputy, a continued underground
stream of backbiting and insinuation going home against
him. Spenser did not forget this, when in the *Faery
Queen* he shadowed forth Lord Grey's career in the
adventures of Arthegal, the great Knight of Justice, met
on his return home from his triumphs by the hags, Envy
and Detraction, and the braying of the hundred tongues
of the Blatant Beast. Irish lords and partisans, calling
themselves loyal, when they could not get what they
wanted, or when he threatened them for their insincerity
or insolence, at once wrote to England. His English
colleagues, civil and military, were his natural rivals or
enemies, ever on the watch to spy out and report,
if necessary, to misrepresent, what was questionable or
unfortunate in his proceedings. Permanent officials like
Archbishop Adam Loftus the Chancellor, or Treasurer
Wallop, or Secretary Fenton, knew more than he did;
they corresponded directly with the ministers; they knew
that they were expected to keep a strict watch on his
expenditure; and they had no scruple to send home complaints against him behind his back, as they did against
one another. A secretary in Dublin like Geoffrey Fenton
is described as a moth in the garment of every Deputy.
Grey himself complains of the underhand work; he cannot
prevent "backbiters' report:" he has found of late "very
suspicious dealing amongst all his best esteemed associates;" he "dislikes not to be informed of the charges
against him." In fact, they were accusing him of one of
the gravest sins of which a Deputy could be guilty; they
were writing home that he was lavishing the forfeited
estates among his favourites, under pretence of rewarding
service, to the great loss and permanent damage of her

Majesty's revenue ; and they were forwarding plans for
commissions to distribute these estates, of which the
Deputy should not be a member.

He had the common fate of those who accepted great
responsibilities under the Queen. He was expected to do
very hard tasks with insufficient means, and to receive
more blame where he failed than thanks where he succeeded. He had every one, English and Irish, against him
in Ireland, and no one for him in England. He was driven
to violence because he wanted strength ; he took liberties
with forfeitures belonging to the Queen because he had no
other means of rewarding public services. It is not easy
to feel much sympathy for a man who, brave and public
spirited as he was, could think of no remedy for the miseries
of Ireland but wholesale bloodshed. Yet, compared with
the resident officials who caballed against him, and who
got rich on these miseries, the Wallops and Fentons of
the Irish Council, this stern Puritan, so remorseless in
what he believed to be his duty to his Queen and his
faith, stands out as an honest and faithful public servant
of a Government which seemed hardly to know its own
mind, which vacillated between indulgence and severity,
and which hampered its officers by contradictory policies,
ignorant of their difficulties, and incapable of controlling
the supplies for a costly and wasteful war. Lord Grey's
strong hand, though incapable of reaching the real causes
of Irish evils, undoubtedly saved the country at a moment
of serious peril, and once more taught lawless Geraldines,
and Eustaces, and Burkes the terrible lesson of English
power. The work which he had half done in crushing
Desmond was soon finished by Desmond's hereditary
rival, Ormond ; and under the milder, but not more
popular, rule of his successor, the proud and irritable Sir

John Perrot, Ireland had for a few years the peace which
consisted in the absence of a definite rebellion, till Tyrone
began to stir in 1595, and Perrot went back a disgraced
man, to die a prisoner in the Tower.

Lord Grey left behind him unappeasable animosities,
and returned to meet jealous rivals and an ill-satisfied
mistress. But he had left behind one whose admiration
and reverence he had won, and who was not afraid to take
care of his reputation. Whether Spenser went back with
his patron or not in 1582, he was from henceforth mainly
resident in Ireland. Lord Grey's administration, and the
principles on which it had been carried on, had made a
deep impression on Spenser's mind. His first ideal had
been Philip Sidney, the attractive and all-accomplished
gentleman,—

> The President
> Of noblesse and of chevalrie,—

And to the end the pastoral Colin Clout, for he ever
retained his first poetic name, was faithful to his ideal.
But in the stern Proconsul, under whom he had become
hardened into a keen and resolute colonist, he had come
in contact with a new type of character ; a governor under
the sense of duty, doing the roughest of work in the
roughest of ways. In Lord Grey, he had this character,
not as he might read of it in books, but acting out its
qualities in present life, amid the unexpected emergencies,
the desperate alternatives, the calls for instant decision,
the pressing necessities and the anxious hazards, of a
course full of uncertainty and peril. He had before his
eyes day by day, fearless, unshrinking determination, in a
hateful and most unpromising task. He believed that he
saw a living example of strength, manliness, and noble-

ness ; of unsparing and unswerving zeal for order and
religion, and good government ; of single-hearted devotion to truth and right, and to the Queen. Lord Grey
grew at last, in the poet's imagination, into the image and
representative of perfect and masculine justice. When
Spenser began to enshrine in a great allegory his ideas
of human life and character, Lord Grey supplied the
moral features, and almost the name, of one of its chief
heroes. Spenser did more than embody his memory in
poetical allegories. In Spenser's *View of the present State
of Ireland*, written some years after Lord Grey's death, he
gives his mature, and then at any rate, disinterested appro-
bation of Lord Grey's administration, and his opinion of
the causes of its failure. He kindles into indignation
when " most untruly and maliciously, those evil tongues
backbite and slander the sacred ashes of that most just
and honourable personage, whose least virtue, of many
most excellent, which abounded in his heroical spirit, they
were never able to aspire unto."

Lord Grey's patronage had brought Spenser into the
public service; perhaps that patronage, the patronage of a
man who had powerful enemies, was the cause that Spenser's preferments, after Lord Grey's recall, were on so
moderate a scale. The notices which we glean from indirect sources about Spenser's employment in Ireland are
meagre enough, but they are distinct. They show him as
a subordinate public servant, of no great account, but yet,
like other public servants in Ireland, profiting, in his
degree, by the opportunities of the time. In the spring
following Lord Grey's arrival (March 22, 1581), Spenser
was appointed Clerk of Decrees and Recognizances in the
Irish Court of Chancery, retaining his place as Secretary
to the Lord-Deputy, in which character his signature some-

times appears in the Irish Records, certifying State documents sent to England. This office is said by Fuller to have been a "lucrative" one. In the same year he received a lease of the Abbey and Manor of Enniscorthy, in the County of Wexford. Enniscorthy was an important post in the network of English garrisons, on one of the roads from Dublin to the South. He held it but for a short time. It was transferred by him to a citizen of Wexford, Richard Synot, an agent, apparently, of the powerful Sir Henry Wallop, the Treasurer; and it was soon after transferred by Synot to his patron, an official who secured to himself a large share of the spoils of Desmond's rebellion. Further, Spenser's name appears, in a list of persons (January, 1582), among whom Lord Grey had distributed some of the forfeited property of the rebels—a list sent home by him in answer to charges of waste and damage to the Queen's revenue, busily urged against him in Ireland by men like Wallop and Fenton, and readily listened to by English ministers like Burghley, who complained that Ireland was a "gulf of consuming treasure." The grant was mostly to persons active in service, among others one to Wallop himself; and a certain number of smaller value to persons of Lord Grey's own household. There, among yeomen ushers, gentlemen ushers, gentlemen serving the Lord-Deputy, and Welshmen and Irishmen with uncouth names, to whom small gratifications had been allotted out of the spoil, we read—" the lease of a house in Dublin belonging to [Lord] Baltinglas for six years to come to Edmund Spenser, one of the Lord-Deputy's Secretaries, valued at 5*l*." . . . " of a 'custodiam' of John Eustace's [one of Baltinglas' family] land of the Newland to Edmund Spenser, one of the Lord-Deputy's Secretaries." In July, 1586, when every one

was full of the project for "planting" Munster, he was
still in Dublin, for he addresses from thence a sonnet to
Gabriel Harvey. In March, 158$\frac{3}{9}$, we find the following,
in a list of officers on the establishment of the province
of Munster, which the government was endeavouring to
colonize from the west of England: "Lodovick Briskett,
clerk to the council (at 20*l.* per annum), 13*l.* 6*s.* 8*d.* (this
is exercised by one Spenser, as deputy for the said Briskett,
to whom (i. e. Briskett) it was granted by patent 6 Nov. 25
Eliz. (1583)." (*Carew MSS.*) Bryskett was a man much
employed in Irish business. He had been Clerk to the
Irish Council, had been a correspondent of Burghley and
Walsingham, and had aspired to be Secretary of State
when Fenton obtained the post : possibly in disappointment, he had retired, with an office which he exercised by
deputy, to his lands in Wexford. He was a poet, and a
friend of Spenser's : and it may have been by his interest
with the dispensers of patronage, that "one Spenser,"
who had been his deputy, succeeded to his office.

In this position Spenser was brought into communica-
tion with the powerful English chiefs on the Council of
Munster, and also with the leading men among the
Undertakers as they were called, among whom more
than half a million of acres of the escheated and desolate
lands of the fallen Desmond were to be divided, on
condition of each Undertaker settling on his estate a
proportionate number of English gentlemen, yeomen,
artisans and labourers with their families, who were to
bring the ruined province into order and cultivation. The
President and Vice-President of the Council were the two
Norreys, John and Thomas, two of the most gallant of
a gallant family. The project for the planting of Munster had been originally started before the rebellion, in

1568. It had been one of the causes of the rebellion;
but now that Desmond was fallen, it was revived. It
had been received in England with favour and hope.
Men of influence and enterprise, Sir Christopher Hatton,
Walsingham, Walter Ralegh, had· embarked in it: and
the government had made an appeal to the English
country gentlemen to take advantage of this new opening
for their younger sons, and to send them over at the head
of colonies from the families of their tenants and depen-
dants, to occupy a rich and beautiful land on easy terms
of rent. In the Western Counties, north and south, the
appeal had awakened interest. In the list of Undertakers are found Cheshire and Lancashire names, Stanley, Fleetwood, Molyneux: and a still larger number
for Somerset, Devon, and Dorset, Popham, Rogers, Coles,
Ralegh, Chudleigh, Champernown. The plan of settlement was carefully and methodically traced out. The
province was surveyed as well as it could be under great
difficulties. Maps were made which Lord Burghley an-
notated. "Seignories" were created of varying size,
12,000, 8000, 6000, 4000 acres, with corresponding
obligations as to the number and class of farms and
inhabitants in each. Legal science in England was to
protect titles by lengthy patents and leases; administra-
tive watchfulness and firmness were to secure them in
Ireland. Privileges of trade were granted to the Undertakers: they were even allowed to transport coin out of
England to Ireland: and a long respite was granted them
before the Crown was to claim its rents. Strict rules
were laid down to keep the native Irish out of the English
lands and from intermarrying with the English families.
In this partition, Seignories were distributed by the
Undertakers among themselves with the free careless-

ness of men dividing the spoil. The great people, like
Hatton and Ralegh, were to have their two or three
Seignories : the county of Cork with its nineteen
Seignories is assigned to the gentleman undertakers
from Somersetshire. The plan was an ambitious and
tempting one. But difficulties soon arose. The gentleman undertakers were not in a hurry to leave England
even on a visit to their desolate and dangerous seignories in Munster. The "planting" did not thrive. The
Irish were inexhaustible in raising legal obstacles and
in giving practical annoyance. Claims and titles were
hard to discover or to extinguish. Even the very
attainted and escheated lands were challenged by virtue
of settlements made before the attainders. The result
was that a certain number of Irish estates were added
to the possessions of a certain number of English families.
But Munster was not planted. Burghley's policy,
and Walsingham's resolution, and Ralegh's daring inventiveness were alike baffled by the conditions of a
problem harder than the peopling of America or the conquest of India. Munster could not be made English.
After all its desolation, it reverted in the main to its
Irish possessors.

Of all the schemes and efforts which accompanied
the attempt, and the records of which fill the Irish State
papers of those years, Spenser was the near and close
spectator. He was in Dublin and on the spot, as Clerk of
the Council of Munster. And he had become acquainted,
perhaps, by this time, had formed a friendship, with
Walter Ralegh, one of the most active men in Irish business, whose influence was rising wherever he was becoming
known. Most of the knowledge which Spenser thus
gathered, and of the impressions which a practical hand-

ling of Irish affairs had left on him, was embodied in his interesting work, written several years later—*A View of the present State of Ireland*. But his connexion with Munster not unnaturally brought him also an accession of fortune. When Ralegh and the "Somersetshire men" were dividing among them the County of Cork, the Clerk of the Council was remembered by some of his friends. He was admitted among the Undertakers. His name appears in the list, among great statesmen and captains with their seignories of 12,000 acres, as holding a grant of some 3000. It was the manor and castle of Kilcolman, a ruined house of the Desmonds, under the Galtee Hills. It appears to have been first assigned to another person.[5] But it came at last into Spenser's hands, probably in 1586 ; and henceforward, this was his abode and his home.

Kilcolman Castle was near the high road between Mallow and Limerick, about three miles from Buttevant and Doneraile, in a plain at the foot of the last western falls of the Galtee range, watered by a stream now called the Awbeg, but which he celebrates under the name of the Mulla. In Spenser's time it was probably surrounded with woods. The earlier writers describe it as a pleasant abode with fine views, and so Spenser celebrated its natural beauties. The more recent accounts are not so favourable. "Kilcolman," says the writer in Murray's Handbook, "is a small peel tower,with cramped and dark rooms, a form which every gentleman's house assumed in turbulent times. It is situated on the margin of a small lake, and, it must be confessed, overlooking an extremely dreary tract of country." It was in the immediate neigh-

[5] Carew MSS. Calendar, 1587, p. 449. Cf. Irish Papers ; Calendar, 1587, p. 309, 450.

bourhood of the wild country to the north, half forest, half bog, the wood and hill of Aharlo, or Arlo, as Spenser writes it, which was the refuge and the "great fastness" of the Desmond rebellion. It was amid such scenes, amid such occupations, in such society and companionship, that the poet of the *Faery Queen* accomplished as much of his work as was given him to do. In one of his later poems, he thus contrasts the peace of England with his own home :—

> No wayling there nor wretchednesse is heard,
> No bloodie issues nor no leprosies,
> No griesly famine, nor no raging sweard,
> No nightly bordrags [= border ravage], nor no hue and cries;
> The shepheards there abroad may safely lie,
> On hills and downes, withouten dread or daunger:
> No ravenous wolves the good mans hope destroy,
> Nor outlawes fell affray the forest raunger.

CHAPTER IV.

[1580—1590.]

THE *Faery Queen* is heard of very early in Spenser's literary course. We know that in the beginning of 1580, the year in which Spenser went to Ireland, something under that title had been already begun and submitted to Gabriel Harvey's judgment; and that among other literary projects, Spenser was intending to proceed with it. But beyond the mere name, we know nothing, at this time, of Spenser's proposed *Faery Queen*. Harvey's criticisms on it tell us nothing of its general plan or its numbers. Whether the first sketch had been decided upon, whether the new stanza, Spenser's original creation, and its peculiar beauty and instrument, had yet been invented by him, while he had been trying experiments in metre in the *Shepherd's Calendar*, we have no means of determining. But he took the idea with him to Ireland; and in Ireland he pursued it and carried it out.

The first authentic account which we have of the composition of the *Faery Queen*, is in a pamphlet written by Spenser's friend and predecessor in the service of the Council of Munster, Ludowick Bryskett, and inscribed to Lord Grey of Wilton: a *Discourse of Civil Life*, published in 1606. He describes a meeting of friends at his

G

cottage near Dublin, and a conversation that took place
on the "ethical" part of moral philosophy. The company consisted of some of the principal Englishmen
employed in Irish affairs, men whose names occur continually in the copious correspondence in the Rolls and at
Lambeth. There was Long, the Primate of Armagh;
there were Sir Robert Dillon, the Chief Justice of the
Common Pleas, and Dormer, the Queen's Solicitor; and
there were soldiers, like Thomas Norreys, then Vice-President of Munster, under his brother John Norreys; Sir
Warham Sentleger, on whom had fallen so much of the
work in the South of Ireland, and who at last, like
Thomas Norreys, fell in Tyrone's rebellion; Captain
Christopher Carleil, Walsingham's son-in-law, a man who
had gained great distinction on land and sea, not only
in Ireland, but in the Low Countries, in France, and at
Carthagena and San Domingo; and Captain Nicholas
Dawtry, the Seneschal of Clandeboy, in the troublesome
Ulster country, afterwards "Captain" of Hampshire at
the time of the Armada. It was a remarkable party.
The date of this meeting must have been after the
summer of 1584, at which time Long was made Primate,
and before the beginning of 1588, when Dawtry was in
Hampshire. The extract is so curious, as a picture of
the intellectual and literary wants and efforts of the
times, especially amid the disorders of Ireland, and as a
statement of Spenser's purpose in his poem, that an
extract from it deserves to be inserted, as it is given in
Mr. Todd's _Life of Spenser_, and repeated in that by
Mr. Hales.

"Herein do I greatly envie," writes Bryskett, " the happiness
of the Italians, who have in their mother-tongue late writers
that have, with a singular easie method taught all that Plato

and Aristotle have confusedly or obscurely left written. Of
which, some I have begun to reade with no small delight; as
Alexander Piccolomini, Gio. Baptista Giraldi, and Guazzo; all
three having written upon the Ethick part of Morall Philosophie
both exactly and perspicuously. And would God that some
of our countrimen would shew themselves so wel affected to the
good of their countrie (whereof one principall and most important part consisteth in the instructing men to vertue), as to
set downe in English the precepts of those parts of Morall
Philosophy, whereby our youth might, without spending so
much time as the learning of those other languages require,
speedily enter into the right course of vertuous life.

"In the meane while I must struggle with those bookes
which I vnderstand and content myselfe to plod upon them, in
hope that God (who knoweth the sincerenesse of my desire) will
be pleased to open my vnderstanding, so as I may reape that
profit of my reading, which I trauell for. Yet is there *a gentleman in this company*, whom I have had often a purpose to
intreate, that as his liesure might serue him, he would vouchsafe to spend some time with me to instruct me in some hard
points which I cannot of myselfe understand; *knowing him to
be not onely perfect in the Greek tongue, but also very well read
in Philosophie, both morall and naturall*. Neuertheless such
is my bashfulness, as I neuer yet durst open my mouth to
disclose this my desire vnto him, though I have not wanted
some hartning thereunto from himselfe. For of loue and kind-
nes to me, *he encouraged me long sithens to follow the reading
of the Greeke tongue, and offered me his helpe to make me
vnderstand it*. But now that so good an opportunitie is offered
vnto me, to satisfie in some sort my desire; I thinke I should
commit a great fault, not to myselfe alone, but to all this
company, if I should not enter my request thus farre, as to
moue him to spend this time which we have now destined to
familiar discourse and conuersation, in declaring vnto us the
great benefits which men obtaine by the knowledge of Morall
Philosophie, and in making us to know what the same is, what
be the parts thereof, whereby vertues are to be distinguished
from vices; and finally that he will be pleased to run ouer in

such order as he shall thinke good, such and so many principles
and rules thereof, as shall serue not only for my better instruc-
tion, but also for the contentment and satisfaction of you al.
For I nothing doubt, but that euery one of you will be glad to
heare so profitable a discourse and thinke the time very wel
spent wherin so excellent a knowledge shal be reuealed unto
you, from which euery one may be assured to gather some fruit
as wel as myselfe.

Therefore (said I), turning myselfe to *M. Spenser*, It is you
sir, to whom it pertaineth to shew yourselfe courteous now
unto vs all and to make vs all beholding unto you for the
pleasure and profit which we shall gather from your speeches,
if you shall vouchsafe to open unto vs the goodly cabinet, in
which this excellent treasure of vertues lieth locked up from
the vulgar sort. And thereof in the behalfe of all as for myselfe, I do most earnestly intreate you not to say vs nay. Vnto
which wordes of mine euery man applauding most with like
words of request and the rest with gesture and countenances
expressing as much, *M. Spenser* answered in this maner :

Though it may seeme hard for me, to refuse the request
made by you all, whom euery one alone, I should for many re-
spects be willing to gratifie; yet as the case standeth, I doubt not
but with the consent of the most part of you, I shall be excused
at this time of this taske which would be laid vpon me; for sure
I am, that it is not vnknowne unto you, that I haue alreedy
vndertaken a work tending to the same effect, which is in
heroical verse under the title of a *Faerie Queene* to represent
all the moral vertues, assigning to euery vertue a Knight to be
the patron and defender of the same, in whose actions and
feates of arms and chiualry the operations of that vertue,
whereof he is the protector, are to be expressed, and the vices
and unruly appetites that oppose themselves against the same,
to be beaten down and ouercome. Which work, *as I haue
already well entred into*, if God shall please to spare me life
that I may finish it according to my mind, your wish (*M.
Bryskett*) will be in some sort accomplished, though perhaps
not so effectually as you could desire. And the same may very
well serue for my excuse, if at this time I craue to be forborne

in this your request, since any discourse, that I might make
thus on the sudden in such a subject would be but simple, and
little to your satisfactions. For it would require good aduise-
ment and premeditation for any man to vndertake the declara-
tion of these points that you have proposed, containing in effect
the Ethicke part of Morall Philosophie. Whereof since I haue
taken in hand to discourse at large in my poeme before spoken,
I hope the expectation of that work may serue to free me at
this time from speaking in that matter, notwithstanding your
motion and all your intreaties. But I will tell you how I
thinke by himselfe he may very well excuse my speech, and yet
satisfie all you in this matter. I haue seene (as he knoweth)
a translation made by himselfe out of the Italian tongue of a
dialogue comprehending all the Ethick part of Moral Philosophy written by one of those three he formerly mentioned,
and that is by *Giraldi* vnder the title of a Dialogue of Ciuil
life. If it please him to bring us forth that translation to be
here read among vs, or otherwise to deliuer to us, as his memory
may serue him, the contents of the same; he shal (I warrant
you) satisfie you all at the ful, and himselfe wil haue no cause
but to thinke the time well spent in reuiewing his labors,
especially in the company of so many his friends, who may
thereby reape much profit, and the translation happily fare the
better by some mending it may receiue in the perusing, as all
writings else may do by the often examination of the same.
Neither let it trouble him that I so turne ouer to him againe
the taske he wold haue put me to; for it falleth out fit for him
to verifie the principall of all this Apologie, euen now made for
himselfe; because thereby it will appeare that he hath not
withdrawne himselfe from seruice of the state to liue idle or
wholly priuate to himselfe, but hath spent some time in doing
that which may greatly benefit others, and hath serued not a
little to the bettering of his owne mind, and increasing of his
knowledge; though he for modesty pretend much ignorance,
and pleade want in wealth, much like some rich beggars, who
either of custom, or for couetousnes, go to begge of others
those things whereof they haue no want at home.

With this answer of *M. Spensers* it seemed that all the

company were wel satisfied, for after some few speeches whereby
they had shewed an extreme longing after his worke of the
*Fairie Queene, whereof some parcels had been by some of them
seene,* they all began to presse me to produce my translation
mentioned by *M. Spenser* that it might be perused among
them; or else that I should (as near as I could) deliuer unto
them the contents of the same, supposing that my memory
would not much faile me in a thing so studied and advisedly set
downe in writing as a translation must be."

A poet at this time still had to justify his employment by presenting himself in the character of a professed
teacher of morality, with a purpose as definite and formal,
though with a different method, as the preacher in the
pulpit. Even with this profession, he had to encounter
many prejudices, and men of gravity and wisdom shook
their heads at what they thought his idle trifling. But if
he wished to be counted respectable, and to separate himself from the crowd of foolish or licentious rimers, he
must intend distinctly, not merely to interest, but to
instruct, by his new and deep conceits. It was under
the influence of this persuasion that Spenser laid down the
plan of the *Faery Queen*. It was, so he proposed to himself, to be a work on moral, and if time were given him,
political philosophy, composed with as serious a didactic
aim, as any treatise or sermon in prose. He deems it
necessary to explain and excuse his work by claiming for
it this design. He did not venture to send the *Faery
Queen* into the world without also telling the world its
moral meaning and bearing. He cannot trust it to tell its
own story or suggest its real drift. In the letter to Sir
W. Ralegh, accompanying the first portion of it, he
unfolds elaborately the sense of his allegory, as he ex-
pounded it to his friends in Dublin. "To some," he says,

" I know this method will seem displeasant, which had
rather have good discipline delivered plainly by way of
precept, or sermoned at large, as they use, than thus
cloudily enwrapped in allegorical devises." He thought
that Homer and Virgil and Ariosto had thus written
poetry, to teach the world moral virtue and political wisdom. He attempted to propitiate Lord Burghley, who
hated him and his verses, by setting before him in a dedication sonnet, the true intent of his—

> Idle rimes;
> The labour of lost time and wit unstaid;
> Yet if their deeper sense he inly weighed,
> And the dim veil, with which from common view
> Their fairer parts are hid, aside be laid,
> Perhaps not vain they may appear to you.

In earlier and in later times, men do not apologize for
being poets ; and Spenser himself was deceived in giving
himself credit for this direct purpose to instruct, when
he was really following the course marked out by his
genius. But he only conformed to the curious utili-
tarian spirit which pervaded the literature of the time.
Readers were supposed to look everywhere for a moral to
be drawn, or a lesson to be inculcated, or some practical
rules to be avowedly and definitely deduced; and they could
not yet take in the idea that the exercise of the specu-
lative and imaginative faculties may be its own end, and
may have indirect influences and utilities even greater
than if it was guided by a conscious intention to be
edifying and instructive.

The first great English poem of modern times, the first
creation of English imaginative power since Chaucer, and
like Chaucer so thoroughly and characteristically English,
was not written in England. Whatever Spenser may have

done to it before he left England with Lord Grey, and
whatever portions of earlier composition may have been
used and worked up into the poem as it went on, the
bulk of the *Faery Queen*, as we have it, was composed in
what to Spenser and his friends was almost a foreign land
—in the conquered and desolated wastes of wild and
barbarous Ireland.   It is a feature of his work on which
Spenser himself dwells.   In the verses which usher in
his poem, addressed to the great men of Elizabeth's court,
he presents his work to the Earl of Ormond, as

> The wild fruit which salvage soil hath bred;
> Which being through long wars left almost waste,
> With brutish barbarism is overspread;—

and in the same strain to Lord Grey, he speaks of his "rude
rimes, the which a rustic muse did weave, in salvage soil."
It is idle to speculate what difference of form the *Faery
Queen* might have received, if the design had been
carried out in the peace of England and in the society of
London.   But it is certain that the scene of trouble and
danger in which it grew up greatly affected it.   This may
possibly account, though it is questionable, for the loose-
ness of texture, and the want of accuracy and finish
which is sometimes to be seen in it.   Spenser was a
learned poet; and his poem has the character of the work
of a man of wide reading, but without books to verify
or correct.   It cannot be doubted that his life in Ireland added to the force and vividness with which
Spenser wrote.   In Ireland, he had before his eyes continually, the dreary world which the poet of knight
errantry imagines.   There men might in good truth
travel long through wildernesses and "great woods" given
over to the outlaw and the ruffian.   There the avenger

of wrong need seldom want for perilous adventure and
the occasion for quelling the oppressor.   There the armed
and unrelenting hand of right was but too truly the
only substitute for law.   There might be found in most
certain and prosaic reality, the ambushes, the disguises,
the treacheries, the deceits and temptations, even the supposed witchcrafts and enchantments, against which the
fairy champions of the virtues have to be on their guard.
In Ireland, Englishmen saw, or at any rate thought they
saw, a universal conspiracy of fraud against righteousness,
a universal battle going on between error and religion,
between justice and the most insolent selfishness.   They
found there every type of what was cruel, brutal, loathsome.   They saw everywhere men whose business it was
to betray and destroy, women whose business it was to
tempt and ensnare and corrupt.   They thought that
they saw too, in those who waged the Queen's wars,
all forms of manly and devoted gallantry, of noble
generosity, of gentle strength, of knightly sweetness and
courtesy.   There were those, too, who failed in the hour
of trial; who were the victims of temptation or of the
victorious strength of evil.   Besides the open or concealed
traitors, the Desmonds, and Kildares, and O'Neales,
there were the men who were entrapped and overcome,
and the men who disappointed hopes, and became
recreants to their faith and loyalty; like Sir William
Stanley, who, after a brilliant career in Ireland, turned
traitor and apostate, and gave up Deventer and his Irish
bands to the King of Spain.

The realities of the Irish wars and of Irish social and
political life gave a real subject, gave body and form to
the allegory.   There in actual flesh and blood were
enemies to be fought with by the good and true.   There

in visible fact were the vices and falsehoods, which Arthur
and his companions were to quell and punish. There in
living truth were *Sansfoy*, and *Sansloy*, and *Sansjoy ;*
there were *Orgoglio* and *Grantorto*, the witcheries of
Acrasia and *Phœdria*, the insolence of *Briana* and *Crudor*.
And there, too, were real Knights of goodness and the
Gospel—Grey, and Ormond, and Ralegh, the Norreyses,
St. Leger, and Maltby—on a real mission from Gloriana's
noble realm to destroy the enemies of truth and virtue.

The allegory bodies forth the trials which beset the
life of man in all conditions and at all times. But
Spenser could never have seen in England such a
strong and perfect image of the allegory itself—with
the wild wanderings of its personages, its daily chances
of battle and danger, its hairbreadth escapes, its strange
encounters, its prevailing anarchy and violence, its normal
absence of order and law—as he had continually and
customarily before him in Ireland. "The curse of God
was so great," writes John Hooker, a contemporary, "and
the land so barren both of man and beast, that whosoever
did travel from one end to the other of all Munster, even
from Waterford to Smerwick, about six score miles, he
should not meet man, woman, or child, saving in cities
or towns, nor yet see any beast, save foxes, wolves or
other ravening beasts." It is the desolation through which
Spenser's knights pursue their solitary way, or join company as they can. Indeed to read the same writer's
account, for instance, of Ralegh's adventures with the
Irish chieftains, his challenges and single combats, his
escapes at fords and woods, is like reading bits of the
Faery Queen in prose. As Spenser chose to write of
knight errantry, his picture of it has doubtless gained in
truth and strength by his very practical experience of

what such life as he describes must be.   The *Faery Queen*
might almost be called the Epic of the English wars in
Ireland under Elizabeth, as much as the Epic of English
virtue and valour at the same period.

At the Dublin meeting described by Bryskett, some time
later than 1584, Spenser had already "well entered into"
his work.   In 1589, he came to England, bringing with
him the first three books ; and early in 1590, they were
published.   Spenser himself has told us the story of this
first appearance of the *Faery Queen*.   The person who
discovered the extraordinary work of genius which was
growing up amid the turbulence and misery and despair of
Ireland, and who once more brought its author into the
centre of English life, was Walter Ralegh.   Ralegh had
served through much of the Munster war.   He had shown
in Ireland some of the characteristic points of his nature,
which made him at once the glory and shame of English
manhood.   He had begun to take a prominent·place in
any business in which he engaged.   He had shown his
audacity, his self-reliance, his resource, and some signs of
that boundless but prudent ambition which marked his
career.   He had shown that freedom of tongue, that
restless and high-reaching inventiveness, and that tenacity
of opinion, which made him a difficult person for others
to work with.   Like so many of the English captains,
he hated Ormond, and saw in his feud with the
Desmonds the real cause of the hopeless disorder of
Munster.   But also he incurred the displeasure and
suspicion of Lord Grey, who equally disliked the great
Irish Chief, but who saw in the "plot" which Ralegh
sent to Burghley for the pacification of Munster, an
adventurer's impracticable and self-seeking scheme.   "I
must be plain," he writes, "I like neither his carriage

nor his company." Ralegh had been at Smerwick: he
had been in command of one of the bands put in by
Lord Grey to do the execution. On Lord Grey's departure he had become one of the leading persons among
the undertakers for the planting of Munster. He had
secured for himself a large share of the Desmond
lands. In 1587, an agreement among the undertakers
assigned to Sir Walter Ralegh, his associates and tenants,
three seignories of 12,000 acres a-piece, and one of
6000, in Cork and Waterford. But before Lord Grey's
departure, Ralegh had left Ireland, and had found the
true field for his ambition in the English court. From
1582 to 1589, he had shared with Leicester and Hatton
and afterwards with Essex, the special favour of the
Queen. He had become Warden of the Stannaries and
Captain of the Guard. He had undertaken the adventure
of founding a new realm in America under the name of
Virginia. He had obtained grants of monopolies, farms
of wines, Babington's forfeited estates. His own great
ship, which he had built, the Ark Ralegh, had carried
the flag of the High Admiral of England in the glorious
but terrible summer of 1588. He joined in that tremen-
dous sea-chase from Plymouth to the North Sea, when, as
Spenser wrote to Lord Howard of Effingham—

> Those huge castles of Castilian King,
> That vainly threatened kingdoms to displace,
> Like flying doves, ye did before you chase.

In the summer of 1589, Ralegh had been busy, as men
of the sea were then, half Queen's servants, half buccaneers,
in gathering the abundant spoils to be found on the high
seas; and he had been with Sir John Norreys and Sir
Francis Drake in a bootless but not unprofitable expe-

dition to Lisbon. On. his return from the Portugal
voyage his court fortunes underwent a change. Essex,
who had long scorned "that knave Ralegh," was in the
ascendant. Ralegh found the Queen, for some reason
or another, and reasons were not hard to find, offended
and dangerous. He bent before the storm. In the end
of the summer of 1589, he was-in Ireland, looking after
his large seignories, his law-suits with the old proprietors,
his castle at Lismore, and his schemes for turning to
account his woods for the manufacture of pipe staves for
the French and Spanish wine trade.

He visited Spenser, who was his neighbour, at Kilcolman, and the visit led to important consequences. The
record of it and of the events which followed, is preserved
in a curious poem of Spenser's written two or three years
later, and of much interest in regard to Spenser's personal history. Taking up the old pastoral form of the
Shepherd's Calendar, with the familiar rustic names of
the swains who figured in its dialogues,—Hobbinol,
Cuddie, Rosalind, and his own Colin Clout,—he described
under the usual poetical disguise, the circumstances which
once more took him back from Ireland to the court.
The court was the place to which all persons wishing to
push their way in the world were attracted. It was not
only the centre of all power, the source of favours and
honours, the seat of all that swayed the destiny of the
nation. It was the home of refinement, and wit, and
cultivation, the place where eminence of all kinds was
supposed to be collected, and to which all ambitions,
literary as much as political, aspired. It was not only a
royal court; it was also a great club. Spenser's poem
shows us how he had sped there, and the impressions made
on his mind by a closer view of the persons and the ways

of that awful and dazzling scene, which exercised such a
spell upon Englishmen, and which seemed to combine or
concentrate in itself the glory and the goodness of heaven,
and all the baseness and malignity of earth. The occasion
deserved a full celebration ; it was indeed a turning-point
in his life, for it led to the publication of the *Faery
Queen*, and to the immediate and enthusiastic recognition
by the Englishmen of the time of his unrivalled pre-
eminence as a poet. In this poetical record, *Colin Clout's
come home again*, containing in it history, criticism, satire,
personal recollections, love passages, we have the picture
of his recollections of the flush and excitement of those
months which saw the first appearance of the *Faery Queen*.
He describes the interruption of his retired and, as he
paints it, peaceful and pastoral life in his Irish home, by
the appearance of Ralegh, the "Shepherd of the Ocean,"
from "the main sea deep." They may have been thrown
together before. Both had been patronized by Leicester.
Both had been together at Smerwick, and probably in
other passages of the Munster war ; both had served under
Lord Grey, Spenser's master, though he had been no lover
of Ralegh. In their different degrees, Ralegh with his two
or three Seignories of half a county, and Spenser with
his more modest estate, they were embarked in the same
enterprise, the plantation of Munster. But Ralegh now
appeared before Spenser in all the glory of a brilliant
favourite, the soldier, the explorer, the daring sea-captain,
the founder of plantations across the ocean, and withal,
the poet, the ready and eloquent discourser, the true judge
and measurer of what was great or beautiful.

The time, too, was one at once of excitement and repose.
Men felt as they feel after a great peril, a great effort, a
great relief ; as the Greeks did after Salamis and Platæa,

as our fathers did after Waterloo.   In the struggle in the
Channel with the might of Spain, England had recognized
its force and its prospects.   One of those solemn moments
had just passed when men see before them the course of
the world turned one way, when it might have been
turned another.   All the world had been looking out to
see what would come to pass ; and nowhere more eagerly
than in Ireland.   Every one, English and Irish alike,
stood agaze to "see how the game would be played."
The great fleet, as it drew near, "worked wonderfully
uncertain yet calm humours in the people, not daring to
disclose their real intention."   When all was decided,
and the distressed ships were cast away on the western
coast, the Irish showed as much zeal as the English in
fulfilling the orders of the Irish council, to " apprehend
and execute all Spaniards found there of what quality
soever."   These were the impressions under which the
two men met.   Ralegh, at the moment, was under a
cloud.   In the poetical fancy picture set before us—

> His song was all a lamentable lay
> Of great unkindnesse, and of usage hard,
> Of Cynthia the Ladie of the Sea,
> Which from her presence faultlesse him debard.
> And ever and anon, with singults rife,
> He cryed out, to make his undersong ;
> Ah ! my loves queene, and goddesse of my life,
> Who shall me pittie, when thou doest me wrong ?

At Kilcolman, Ralegh became acquainted with what
Spenser had done of the *Faery Queen*.   His rapid and
clear judgment showed him how immeasurably it rose
above all that had yet been produced under the name of
poetry in England.   That alone is sufficient to account
for his eager desire that it should be known in England.
But Ralegh always had an eye to his own affairs, marred

as they so often were by ill-fortune and his own mistakes;
and he may have thought of making his peace with
Cynthia, by reintroducing at Court the friend of Philip
Sidney, now ripened into a poet not unworthy of Gloriana's
greatness.   This is Colin Clout's account :—

> When thus our pipes we both had wearied well,
> (Quoth he) and each an end of singing made,
> He gan to cast great lyking to my lore,
> And great dislyking to my lucklesse lot,
> That banisht had my selfe, like wight forlore,
> Into that waste, where I was quite forgot.
> The which to leave, thenceforth he counseld mee,
> Unmeet for man, in whom was ought regardfull,
> And wend with him, his Cynthia to see :
> Whose grace was great, and bounty most rewardfull ;
> Besides her peerlesse skill in making well,
> And all the ornaments of wondrous wit,
> Such as all womankynd did far excell,
> Such as the world admyr'd, and praised it.
> So what with hope of good, and hate of ill,
> He me perswaded forth with him to fare.
> Nought tooke I with me, but mine oaten quill :
> Small needments else need shepheard to prepare.
> So to the sea we came ; the sea, that is
> A world of waters heaped up on hie,
> Rolling like mountaines in wide wildernesse,
> Horrible, hideous, roaring with hoarse crie.

This is followed by a spirited description of a sea-
voyage, and of that empire of the seas in which, since
the overthrow of the Armada, England and England's
mistress were now claiming to be supreme, and of which
Ralegh was one of the most active and distinguished
officers :—

> And yet as ghastly dreadfull, as it seemes,
> Bold men, presuming life for gaine to sell,
> Dare tempt that gulf, and in those wandring stremes
> Seek waies unknowne, waies leading down to hell.

For, as we stood there waiting on the strond,
Behold ! an huge great vessell to us came,
Dauncing upon the waters back to lond,
As if it scornd the daunger of the same ;
Yet was it but a wooden frame and fraile,
Glewed togither with some subtile matter.
Yet had it armes and wings, and head and taile,
And life to move it selfe upon the water.
Strange thing ! how bold and swift the monster was,
That neither car'd for wind, nor haile, nor raine,
Nor swelling waves, but thorough them did passe
So proudly, that she made them roare againe.
The same aboord us gently did receave,
And without harme us farre away did beare,
So farre that land, our mother, us did leave,
And nought but sea and heaven to us appeare.
Then hartlesse quite, and full of inward feare,
That shepheard I besought to me to tell,
Under what skie, or in what world we were,
In which I saw no living people dwell.
Who, me recomforting all that he might,
Told me that that same was the Regiment
Of a great Shepheardesse, that Cynthia hight,
His liege, his Ladie, and his lifes Regent.

This is the poetical version of Ralegh's appreciation of
the treasure which he had lighted on in Ireland, and of what
he did to make it known to the admiration and delight
of England.   He returned to the Court, and Spenser with
him.   Again, for what reason we know not, he was received into favour.   The poet, who accompanied him,
was brought to the presence of the lady, who saw herself
in " various mirrors,"—Cynthia, Gloriana, Belphœbe, as
she heard him read portions of the great poem which was
to add a new glory to her reign.

" The Shepheard of the Ocean (quoth he)
Unto that Goddesse grace me first enhanced,
And to mine oaten pipe enclin'd her eare,
That she thenceforth therein gan take delight ;

H

And it desir'd at timely houres to heare,
All were my notes but rude and roughly dight;
For not by measure of her owne great mynde,
And wondrous worth, she mott my simple song,
But joyd that country shepheard ought could fynd
Worth harkening to, emongst the learned throng."

He had already too well caught the trick of flattery—
flattery in a degree almost inconceivable to us—which the
fashions of the time, and the Queen's strange self-deceit,
exacted from the loyalty and enthusiasm of Englishmen.
In that art Ralegh was only too apt a teacher. Colin
Clout, in his story of his recollections of the Court, lets
us see how he was taught to think and to speak there :—

But if I her like ought on earth might read,
I would her lyken to a crowne of lillies,
Upon a virgin brydes adorned head,
With Roses dight and Goolds and Daffadillies ;
Or like the circlet of a Turtle true,
In which all colours of the rainbow bee ;
Or like faire Phebes garlond shining new,
In which all pure perfection one may see.
But vaine it is to thinke, by paragone
Of earthly things, to judge of things divine :
Her power, her mercy, her wisdome, none
Can deeme, but who the Godhead can define.
Why then do I, base shepheard, bold and blind,
Presume the things so sacred to prophane ?
More fit it is t' adore, with humble mind,
The image of the heavens in shape humane.

The Queen, who heard herself thus celebrated, celebrated
not only as a semi-divine person, but as herself unrivalled
in the art of "making" or poetry,—" her peerless skill
in making well,"—granted Spenser a pension of 50l. a
year, which, it is said, the prosaic and frugal Lord Treasurer, always hard-driven for money and not caring much
for poets, made difficulties about paying. But the new

poem was not for the Queen's ear only. In the registers
of the Stationers' Company occurs the following entry :—

Primo die Decembris [1589].

Mr. Ponsonbye—Entered for his Copye, a book intytuled the
fayrye Queene dysposed into xij bookes &c., authorysed under
thandes of the Archbishop of Canterbery and bothe the Wardens.

vj^{d.}

Thus, between pamphlets of the hour,—an account of the
Arms of the City Companies on one side, and the last
news from France on the other,—the first of our great
modern English poems was licensed to make its appearance. It appeared soon after, with the date of 1590. It
was not the twelve books, but only the first three. It
was accompanied and introduced, as usual, by a great
host of commendatory and laudatory sonnets and
poems. All the leading personages at Elizabeth's court
were appealed to ; according to their several tastes or their
relations to the poet, they are humbly asked to befriend, or
excuse, or welcome his poetical venture. The list itself
is worth quoting :—Sir Christopher Hatton, then Lord
Chancellor, the Earls of Essex, Oxford, Northumberland,
Ormond, Lord Howard of Effingham, Lord Grey of Wilton,
Sir Walter Ralegh, Lord Burleigh, the Earl of Cumber-
land, Lord Hunsdon, Lord Buckhurst, Walsingham, Sir
John Norris, President of Munster. He addresses Lady
Pembroke, in remembrance of her brother, that "heroic
spirit," "the glory of our days,"

Who first my Muse did lift out of the floor,
To sing his sweet delights in lowly lays.

And he finishes with a sonnet to Lady Carew, one of Sir
John Spencer's daughters, and another to "all the gracious
and beautiful ladies of the Court," in which "the world's

H 2

pride seems to be gathered." There come also congratu-
lations and praises for himself. Ralegh addressed to him
a fine but extravagant sonnet, in which he imagined
Petrarch weeping for envy at the approval of the *Faery
Queen*, while "Oblivion laid him down on Laura's hearse,"
and even Homer trembled for his fame. Gabriel Harvey
revoked his judgment on the *Elvish Queen*, and not without some regret for less ambitious days in the past, cheered
on his friend in his noble enterprise. Gabriel Harvey
has been so much, and not without reason, laughed at,
and yet his verses welcoming the *Faery Queen* are so
full of true and warm friendship, and of unexpected refinement and grace, that it is but just to cite them. In
the eyes of the world he was an absurd personage : but
Spenser saw in him perhaps his worthiest and trustiest
friend. A generous and simple affection has almost got
the better in them of pedantry and false taste.

> Collyn, I see, by thy new taken taske,
>   Some sacred fury hath enricht thy braynes,
> That leades thy muse in haughty verse to maske,
>   And loath the layes that longs to lowly swaynes ;
> That lifts thy notes from Shepheardes unto kinges :
> So like the lively Larke that mounting singes.
>
> Thy lovely Rosolinde seemes now forlorne,
>   And all thy gentle flockes forgotten quight :
> Thy chaunged hart now holdes thy pypes in scorne,
>   Those prety pypes that did thy mates delight ;
> Those trusty mates, that loved thee so well ;
> Whom thou gav'st mirth, as they gave thee the bell.
>
> Yet, as thou earst with thy sweete roundelayes
>   Didst stirre to glee our laddes in homely bowers ;
> So moughtst thou now in these refyned layes
>   Delight the daintie eares of higher powers :
> And so mought they, in their deepe skanning skill,
> Alow and grace our Collyns flowing quyll.

And faire befall that *Faery Queene* of thine,
  In whose faire eyes love linckt with vertue sittes ;
Enfusing, by those bewties fyers devyne,
  Such high conceites into thy humble wittes,
As raised hath poore pastors oaten reedes
From rustick tunes, to chaunt heroique deedes.

So mought thy *Redcrosse Knight* with happy hand
  Victorious be in that faire Ilands right,
Which thou dost vayle in Type of Faery land,
  Elizas blessed field, that *Albion* hight :
That shieldes her friendes, and warres her mightie foes,
Yet still with people, peace, and plentie flowes.

But (jolly shepheard) though with pleasing style
  Thou feast the humour of the Courtly trayne,
Let not conceipt thy setled sence beguile,
  Ne daunted be through envy or disdaine.
Subject thy dome to her Empyring spright,
From whence thy Muse, and all the world, takes light.
                                    HOBYNOLL.

And to the Queen herself Spenser presented his work,
in one of the boldest dedications perhaps ever penned :—

                        To
    The Most High, Mightie, and Magnificent
                    Empresse,
  Renowmed for piety, vertve, and all gratiovs government,
                  ELIZABETH,
                By the Grace of God,
  Qveene of England, Fravnce, and Ireland, and of Virginia,
            Defendovr of the Faith, &c.
            Her most hvmble Servavnt
              EDMVND SPENSER,
              Doth, in all hvmilitie,
          Dedicate, present, and consecrate
                These his labovrs,
          To live with the eternitie of her fame.

"To live with the eternity of her fame,"—the claim
was a proud one, but it has proved a prophecy. The pub-

lication of the *Faery Queen* placed him at once and for
his lifetime at the head of all living English poets.   The
world of his day immediately acknowledged the charm
and perfection of the new work of art which had taken
it by surprise.   As far as appears, it was welcomed
heartily and generously.   Spenser speaks in places of
envy and detraction, and he, like others, had no doubt
his rivals and enemies.   But little trace of censure appears, except in the stories about Burghley's dislike of
him, as an idle rimer, and perhaps as a friend of his
opponents.   But his brother poets, men like Lodge and
Drayton, paid honour, though in quaint phrases, to the
learned Colin, the reverend Colin, the excellent and
cunning Colin.   A greater than they, if we may trust
his editors, takes him as the representative of poetry,
which is so dear to him.

> If music and sweet poetry agree,
> As they must needs, the sister and the brother,
> Then must the love be great 'twixt thee and me,
> Because thou lov'st the one, and I the other.
> *Dowland* to thee is dear, whose heavenly touch
> Upon the lute doth ravish human sense;
> *Spenser* to me, whose deep conceit is such
> As passing all conceit, needs no defence.
> Thou lov'st to hear the sweet melodious sound
> That Phœbus' lute, the queen of music, makes;
> And I in deep delight am chiefly drown'd
> Whenas himself to singing he betakes.
> One god is god of both, as poets feign;
> One knight loves both, and both in thee remain.
>   (*Shakespere*, in the *Passionate Pilgrim*, 1599.)

Even the fierce pamphleteer, Thomas Nash, the scourge
and torment of poor Gabriel Harvey, addresses Harvey's
friend as heavenly Spenser, and extols "the Faery
Singers' stately tuned verse."   Spenser's title to be the

" Poet of poets," was at once acknowledged as by acclama-
tion. And he himself has no difficulty in accepting his
position. In some lines on the death of a friend's wife,
whom he laments and praises, the idea presents itself
that the great queen may not approve of her Shepherd
wasting his lays on meaner persons ; and he puts into his
friend's mouth a deprecation of her possible jealousy.
The lines are characteristic, both in their beauty and
music, and in the strangeness, in our eyes, of the excuse
made for the poet.

> Ne let Eliza, royall Shepheardesse,
> The praises of my parted love envy,
> For she hath praises in all plenteousnesse
> Powr'd upon her, like showers of Castaly,
> By her own Shepheard, Colin, her owne Shepheard,
> That her with heavenly hymnes doth deifie,
> Of rustick muse full hardly to be betterd.
>
> She is the Rose, the glorie of the day,
> And mine the Primrose in the lowly shade :
> Mine, ah ! not mine ; amisse I mine did say :
> Not mine, but His, which mine awhile her made ;
> Mine to be His, with him to live for ay.
> O that so faire a flower so soone should fade,
> And through untimely tempest fall away !
>
> She fell away in her first ages spring,
> Whil'st yet her leafe was greene, and fresh her rinde,
> And whilst her braunch faire blossomes foorth did bring,
> She fell away against all course of kinde.
> For age to dye is right, but youth is wrong ;
> She fel away like fruit blowne downe with winde.
> Weepe, Shepheard ! weepe, to make my undersong.

Thus in both his literary enterprises, Spenser had been
signally successful. The *Shepherd's Calendar* in 1580 had
immediately raised high hopes of his powers. The *Faery
Queen* in 1590 had more than fulfilled them. In the
interval a considerable change had happened in English

cultivation. Shakespere had come to London, though the
world did not yet know all that he was. Sidney had
published his *Defense of Poesie*, and had written the
Arcadia, though it was not yet published. Marlowe had
begun to write, and others beside him were preparing the
change which was to come on the English Drama. Two
scholars who had shared with Spenser in the bounty of
Robert Nowell were beginning, in different lines, to raise
the level of thought and style. Hooker was beginning to
give dignity to controversy, and to show what English
prose might rise to. Lancelot Andrewes, Spenser's junior
at school and college, was training himself at St. Paul's,
to lead the way to a larger and higher kind of preaching than the English clergy had yet reached. The
change of scene from Ireland to the centre of English
interests, must have been, as Spenser describes it, very
impressive. England was alive with aspiration and effort;
imaginations were inflamed and hearts stirred by the deeds
of men who described with the same energy with which
they acted. Amid such influences, and with such a friend
as Ralegh, Spenser may naturally have been tempted by
some of the dreams of advancement of which Ralegh's
soul was full. There is strong probability, from the
language of his later poems, that he indulged such hopes,
and that they were disappointed. A year after the entry
in the Stationers' Register of the *Faery Queen* (29 Dec.,
1590), Ponsonby, his publisher, entered a volume of
" *Complaints, containing sundry small poems of the World's
Vanity,*" to which he prefixed the following notice.

THE PRINTER TO THE GENTLE READER.

SINCE my late setting foorth of the *Faerie Queene*, finding that
it hath found a favourable passage amongst you, I have sithence

endevoured by all good meanes (for the better encrease and accomplishment of your delights,) to get into my handes such smale Poemes of the same Authors, as I heard were disperst abroad in sundrie hands, and not easie to bee come by, by himselfe; some of them having bene diverslie imbeziled and purloyned from him since his departure over Sea. Of the which I have, by good meanes, gathered togeather these fewe parcels present, which I have caused to bee imprinted altogeather, for that they al seeme to containe like matter of argument in them; being all complaints and meditations of the worlds vanitie, verie grave and profitable.   To which effect I understand that he besides wrote sundrie others, namelie *Ecclesiastes* and *Canticum canticorum* translated, *A senights slumber, The hell of lovers, his Purgatorie,* being all dedicated to Ladies; so as it may seeme he ment them all to one volume.   Besides some other Pamphlets looselie scattered abroad . as *The dying Pellican, The howers of the Lord, The sacrifice of a sinner, The seven Psalmes,* &c., which when I can, either by himselfe or otherwise, attaine too; I meane likewise for your favour sake to set foorth.   In the meane time, praying you gentlie to accept of these, and graciouslie to entertaine the new Poet, *I take leave.*

The collection is a miscellaneous one, both as to subjects and date : it contains among other things, the translations from Petrarch and Du Bellay, which had appeared in Vander Noodt's *Theatre of Worldlings,* in 1569.   But there are also some pieces of later date ; and they disclose not only personal sorrows and griefs, but also an experience which had ended in disgust and disappointment. In spite of Ralegh's friendship, he had found that in the Court he was not likely to thrive.   The two powerful men who had been his earliest friends had disappeared. Philip Sidney had died in 1586 ; Leicester, soon after the destruction of the Armada, in 1588.   And they had been followed (April, 1590) by Sidney's powerful father-in-law, Francis Walsingham.   The death of Leicester, untended,

unlamented, powerfully impressed Spenser, always keenly
alive to the pathetic vicissitudes of human greatness. In
one of these pieces, *The Ruins of Time*, addressed to
Sidney's sister, the Countess of Pembroke, Spenser thus
imagines the death of Leicester,—

> It is not long, since these two eyes beheld
> A mightie Prince, of most renowmed race,
> Whom England high in count of honour held,
> And greatest ones did sue to gaine his grace;
> Of greatest ones he, greatest in his place,
> Sate in the bosome of his Soveraine,
> And *Right and loyall* did his word maintaine.
>
> I saw him die, I saw him die, as one
> Of the meane people, and brought foorth on beare;
> I saw him die, and no man left to mone
> His dolefull fate, that late him loved deare:
> Scarse anie left to close his eylids neare;
> Scarse anie left upon his lips to laie
> The sacred sod, or Requiem to saie.
>
> O! trustless state of miserable men,
> That builde your blis on hope of earthly thing,
> And vainlie thinke your selves halfe happie then,
> When painted faces with smooth flattering
> Doo fawne on you, and your wide praises sing;
> And, when the courting masker louteth lowe,
> Him true in heart and trustie to you trow.

For Sidney, the darling of the time, who had been to
him not merely a cordial friend, but the realized type of
all that was glorious in manhood, and beautiful in character and gifts, his mourning was more than that of a
looker-on at a moving instance of the frailty of greatness.
It was the poet's sorrow for the poet, who had almost
been to him what the elder brother is to the younger.
Both now, and in later years, his affection for one who was
become to him a glorified saint, showed itself in deep and

genuine expression, through the affectations which crowned the "herse" of Astrophel and Philisides. He was persuaded that Sidney's death had been a grave blow to literature and learning. The *Ruins of Time*, and still more the *Tears of the Muses*, are full of lamentations over returning barbarism and ignorance, and the slight account made by those in power of the gifts and the arts of the writer, the poet, and the dramatist. Under what was popularly thought the crabbed and parsimonious administration of Burghley, and with the churlishness of the Puritans, whom he was supposed to foster, it seemed as if the poetry of the time was passing away in chill discouragement. The effect is described in lines which, as we now naturally suppose, and Dryden also thought, can refer to no one but Shakespere. But it seems doubtful whether all this could have been said of Shakespere in 1590. It seems more likely that this also is an extravagant compliment to Philip Sidney, and his masking performances. He was lamented elsewhere under the poetical name of *Willy*. If it refers to him, it was probably written before his death, though not published till after it ; for the lines imply, not that he is literally dead, but that he is in retirement. The expression that he is "dead of late," is explained in four lines below, as "choosing to sit in idle cell," and is one of Spenser's common figures for inactivity or sorrow.[1]

The verses are the lamentations of the Muse of Comedy.

THALIA.

Where be the sweete delights of learning's treasure
That wont with Comick sock to beautefie
The painted Theaters, and fill with pleasure
The listners eyes and eares with melodie ;

---

[1] *v. Colin Clout*, l. 31.   *Astrophel*, l. 175.

In which I late was wont to raine as Queene,
And maske in mirth with Graces well beseene ?

O! all is gone; and all that goodly glee,
Which wont to be the glorie of gay wits,
Is layed abed, and no where now to see ;
And in her roome unseemly Sorrow sits,
With hollow browes and greisly countenaunce,
Marring my joyous gentle dalliaunce.

And him beside sits ugly Barbarisme,
And brutish Ignorance, ycrept of late
Out of dredd darknes of the deepe Abysme,
Where being bredd, he light and heaven does hate :
They in the mindes of men now tyrannize,
And the faire Scene with rudenes foule disguize.

All places they with follie have possest,
And with vaine toyes the vulgare entertaine ;
But me have banished, with all the rest
That whilome wont to wait upon my traine,
Fine Counterfesaunce, and unhurtfull Sport,
Delight, and Laughter, deckt in seemly sort.

All these, and all that els the Comick Stage
With seasoned wit and goodly pleasance graced,
By which mans life in his likest image
Was limned forth, are wholly now defaced ;
And those sweete wits, which wont the like to frame,
Are now despizd, and made a laughing game.

And he, the man whom Nature selfe had made
To mock her selfe, and truth to imitate,
With kindly counter under Mimick shade,
Our pleasant Willy, ah ! *is dead of late;*
With whom all joy and jolly merriment
Is also deaded, and in dolour drent.

*   *   *   *   *

But that same gentle Spirit, from whose pen
Large streames of honnie and sweete Nectar flowe,
Scorning the boldnes of such base-borne men,
Which dare their follies forth so rashlie throwe,
Doth rather choose to sit in idle Cell,
Than so himselfe to mockerie to sell.

But the most remarkable of these pieces is a satirical fable, *Mother Hubberd's Tale of the Ape and Fox*, which may take rank with the satirical writings of Chaucer and Dryden for keenness of touch, for breadth of treatment, for swing and fiery scorn, and sustained strength of sarcasm. By his visit to the Court, Spenser had increased his knowledge of the realities of life. That brilliant Court, with a goddess at its head, and full of charming swains and divine nymphs, had also another side. It was still his poetical heaven. But with that odd insensibility to anomaly and glaring contrasts, which is seen in his time, and perhaps exists at all times, he passed from the celebration of the dazzling glories of Cynthia's Court, into a fierce vein of invective against its treacheries, its vain shows, its unceasing and mean intrigues, its savage jealousies, its fatal rivalries, the scramble there for preferment in Church and State. When it is considered what great persons might easily and naturally have been identified at the time with the *Ape and the Fox*, the confederate impostors, charlatans, and bullying swindlers, who had stolen the lion's skin, and by it mounted to the high places of the State, it seems to be a proof of the indifference of the Court to the power of mere literature, that it should have been safe to write and publish so freely, and so cleverly. Dull Catholic lampoons and Puritan scurrilities did not pass thus unnoticed. They were viewed as dangerous to the State, and dealt with accordingly. The fable contains what we can scarcely doubt to be some of that wisdom which Spenser learnt by his experience of the Court.

> So pitifull a thing is Suters state !
> Most miserable man, whom wicked fate
> Hath brought to Court, to sue for *had-ywist*,
> That few have found, and manie one hath mist !

Full little knowest thou, that hast not tride,
What hell it is in suing long to bide:
To loose good dayes, that might be better spent;
To wast long nights in pensive discontent;
To speed to day, to be put back to morrow;
To feed on hope, to pine with feare and sorrow ;
To have thy Princes grace, yet want her Peeres;
To have thy asking, yet waite manie yeeres;
To fret thy soule with crosses and with cares ;
To eate thy heart through comfortlesse dispaires ;
To fawne, to crowche, to waite, to ride, to ronne,
To spend, to give, to want, to be undonne.
Unhappie wight, borne to disastrous end,
That doth his life in so long tendance spend !
   Who ever leaves sweete home, where meane estate
In safe assurance, without strife or hate,
Findes all things needfull for contentment meeke,
And will to Court for shadowes vaine to seeke,
Or hope to gaine, himselfe will a daw trie :
That curse God send unto mine enemie !

Spenser probably did not mean his characters to fit too
closely to living persons. That might have been dangerous. But it is difficult to believe that he had not
distinctly in his eye a very great personage, the greatest
in England next to the Queen, in the following picture
of the doings of the Fox installed at Court.

But the false Foxe most kindly plaid his part;
For whatsoever mother-wit or arte
Could worke, he put in proofe: no practise slie,
No counterpoint of cunning policie,
No reach, no breach, that might him profit bring,
But he the same did to his purpose wring.
Nought suffered he the Ape to give or graunt,
But through his hand must passe the Fiaunt.
    *   *   *   *   *
He chaffred Chayres in which Churchmen were set,
And breach of lawes to privie ferme did let :
No statute so established might bee,
Nor ordinaunce so needfull, but that hee

Would violate, though not with violence,
Yet under colour of the confidence
The which the Ape repos'd in him alone,
And reckned him the kingdomes corner stone.
And ever, when he ought would bring to pas,
His long experience the platforme was:
And, when he ought not pleasing would put by
The cloke was care of thrift, and husbandry,
For to encrease the common treasures store;
But his owne treasure he encreased more,
And lifted up his loftie towres thereby,
That they began to threat the neighbour sky;
The whiles the Princes pallaces fell fast
To ruine (for what thing can ever last?)
And whilest the other Peeres, for povertie,
Were forst their auncient houses to let lie,
And their olde Castles to the ground to fall,
Which their forefathers, famous over-all,
Had founded for the Kingdome's ornament,
And for their memories long moniment:
But he no count made of Nobilitie,
Nor the wilde beasts whom armes did glorifie,
The Realmes chiefe strength and girlond of the crowne.
All these through fained crimes he thrust adowne,
Or made them dwell in darknes of disgrace;
For none, but whom he list, might come in place.
  Of men of armes he had but small regard,
But kept them lowe, and streigned verie hard.
For men of learning little he esteemed;
His wisdome he above their learning deemed.
As for the rascall Commons, least he cared,
For not so common was his bountie shared.
Let God, (said he) if please, care for the manie,
I for my selfe must care before els anie.
So did he good to none, to manie ill,
So did he all the kingdome rob and pill;
Yet none durst speake, ne none durst of him plaine,
So great he was in grace, and rich through gaine.
Ne would he anie let to have accesse
Unto the Prince, but by his owne addresse,
For all that els did come were sure to faile.

Even at Court, however, the poet finds a contrast to all
this : he had known Philip Sidney, and Ralegh was his
friend.

> Yet the brave Courtier, in whose beauteous thought
> Regard of honour harbours more than ought,
> Doth loath such base condition, to backbite
> Anies good name for envie or despite :
> He stands on tearmes of honourable minde,
> Ne will be carried with the common winde
> Of Courts inconstant mutabilitie,
> Ne after everie tattling fable flie ;
> But heares and sees the follies of the rest,
> And thereof gathers for himselfe the best.
> He will not creepe, nor crouche with fained face,
> But walkes upright with comely stedfast pace,
> And unto all doth yeeld due curtesie ;
> But not with kissed hand belowe the knee,
> As that same Apish crue is wont to doo :
> For he disdaines himselfe t' embase thereto.
> He hates fowle leasings, and vile flatterie,
> Two filthie blots in noble gentrie ;
> And lothefull idlenes he doth detest,
> The canker worme of everie gentle brest.

> Or lastly, when the bodie list to pause,
> His minde unto the Muses he withdrawes :
> Sweete Ladie Muses, Ladies of delight,
> Delights of life, and ornaments of light !
> With whom he close confers with wise discourse,
> Of Natures workes, of heavens continuall course,
> Of forreine lands, of people different,
> Of kingdomes change, of divers gouvernment,
> Of dreadfull battailes of renowned Knights ;
> With which he kindleth his ambitious sprights
> To like desire and praise of noble fame,
> The onely upshot whereto he doth ayme :
> For all his minde on honour fixed is,
> To which he levels all his purposis,
> And in his Princes service spends his dayes,
> Not so much for to gaine, or for to raise

> Himselfe to high degree, as for his grace,
> And in his liking to winne worthie place,
> Through due deserts and comely carriage.

The fable also throws light on the way in which
Spenser regarded the religious parties, whose strife was
becoming loud and threatening.   Spenser is often spoken
of as a Puritan.   He certainly had the Puritan hatred of
Rome ; and in the Church system as it existed in England
he saw many instances of ignorance, laziness, and corruption ; and he agreed with the Puritans in denouncing them.
His pictures of the "formal priest," with his excuses for
doing nothing, his new-fashioned and improved substitutes
for the ornate and also too lengthy ancient service, and his
general ideas of self-complacent comfort, has in it an odd
mixture of Roman Catholic irony with Puritan censure.
Indeed, though Spenser hated with an Englishman's hatred
all that he considered Roman superstition and tyranny, he
had a sense of the poetical impressiveness of the old ceremonial, and the ideas which clung to it, its pomp, its
beauty, its suggestiveness, very far removed from the
iconoclastic temper of the Puritans.   In his *View of the
State of Ireland,* he notes as a sign of its evil condition
the state of the churches, "most of them ruined and even
with the ground," and the rest " so unhandsomely patched
and thatched, that men do even shun the places, for the
uncomeliness thereof."   "The outward form (assure yourself)," he adds, " doth greatly draw the rude people to the
reverencing and frequenting thereof, *whatever some of our
late too nice fools may say*, that there is nothing in the
seemly form and comely order of the church."

> " Ah ! but (said th' Ape) the charge is wondrous great,
> To feede mens soules, and hath an heavie threat."
> " To feed mens soules (quoth he) is not in man ;
> For they must feed themselves, doo what we can.

I

We are but charged to lay the meate before :
Eate they that list, we need to doo no more.
But God it is that feeds them with his grace,
The bread of life powr'd downe from heavenly place.
Therefore said he, that with the budding rod
Did rule the Jewes, *All shalbe taught of God.*
That same hath Jesus Christ now to him raught,
By whom the flock is rightly fed, and taught :
He is the Shepheard, and the Priest is hee ;
We but his shepheard swaines ordain'd to bee.
Therefore herewith doo not your selfe dismay ;
Ne is the paines so great, but beare ye may,
For not so great, as it was wont of yore,
It's now a dayes, ne halfe so streight and sore.
They whilome used duly everie day
Their service and their holie things to say,
At morne and even, besides their Anthemes sweete,
Their penie Masses, and their Complynes meete,
Their Diriges, their Trentals, and their shrifts,
Their memories, their singings, and their gifts.
Now all those needlesse works are laid away ;
Now once a weeke, upon the Sabbath day,
It is enough to doo our small devotion,
And then to follow any merrie motion.
Ne are we tyde to fast, but when we list ;
Ne to weare garments base of wollen twist,
But with the finest silkes us to aray,
That before God we may appeare more gay,
Resembling Aarons glorie in his place :
For farre unfit it is, that person bace
Should with vile cloaths approach Gods majestie,
Whom no uncleannes may approachen nie ;
Or that all men, which anie master serve,
Good garments for their service should deserve ;
But he that serves the Lord of hoasts most high,
And that in highest place, t' approach him nigh,
And all the peoples prayers to present
Before his throne, as on ambassage sent
Both too and fro, should not deserve to weare
A garment better than of wooll or heare.
Beside, we may have lying by our sides
Our lovely Lasses, or bright shining Brides :

We be not tyde to wilfull chastitie,
But have the Gospell of free libertie."

But his weapon is double-edged, and he had not much
more love for

That ungracious crew which feigns demurest grace.

The first prescription which the Priest gives to the
Fox who desires to rise to preferment in the Church is
to win the favour of some great Puritan noble.

First, therefore, when ye have in handsome wise
Your selfe attyred, as you can devise,
Then to some Noble-man your selfe applye,
Or other great one in the worldës eye,
That hath a zealous disposition
To God, and so to his religion.
There must thou fashion eke a godly zeale,
Such as no carpers may contrayre reveale ;
For each thing fained ought more warie bee.
There thou must walke in sober gravitee,
And seeme as Saintlike as Sainte Radegund :
Fast much, pray oft, looke lowly on the ground,
And unto everie one doo curtesie meeke :
These lookes (nought saying) doo a benefice seeke,
And be thou sure one not to lack or long.

But he is impartial, and points out that there are other
ways of rising—by adopting the fashions of the Court,
"facing, and forging, and scoffing, and crouching to
please," and so to "mock out a benefice ;" or else, by
compounding with a patron to give him half the profits,
and in the case of a bishopric, to submit to the alienation
of its manors to some powerful favourite, as the Bishop
of Salisbury had to surrender Sherborn to Sir Walter
Ralegh.   Spenser, in his dedication of *Mother Hubberd's Tale* to one of the daughters of Sir John Spencer,
Lady Compton and Monteagle, speaks of it as "long

sithence composed in the raw conceit of youth." But, whatever this may mean, and it was his way thus to deprecate severe judgments, his allowing the publication of it at this time, shows, if the work itself did not show it, that he was in very serious earnest in his bitter sarcaoms on the base and evil arts which brought success at the Court.

He stayed in England about a year and a half [1590-91], long enough apparently to make up his mind that he had not much to hope for from his great friends, Ralegh and perhaps Essex, who were busy on their own schemes. Ralegh, from whom Spenser might hope most, was just beginning to plunge into that extraordinary career, in the thread of which glory and disgrace, far-sighted and princely public spirit and insatiate private greed, were to be so strangely intertwined. In 1592 he planned the great adventure which astonished London by the fabulous plunder of the Spanish treasure-ships; in the same year he was in the Tower, under the Queen's displeasure for his secret marriage, affecting the most ridiculous despair at her going away from the neighbourhood, and pouring forth his flatteries on this old woman of sixty as if he had no bride of his own to love :—"I that was wont to behold her riding like Alexander, hunting like Diana, walking like Venus; the gentle wind blowing her fair hair about her pure cheeks like a nymph; sometimes, sitting in the shade like a goddess; sometimes, singing like an angel; sometimes, playing like Orpheus—behold the sorrow of this world—once amiss, hath bereaved me of all." Then came the exploration of Guiana, the expedition to Cadiz, the Island voyage [1595—1597]. Ralegh had something else to do than to think of Spenser's fortunes.

Spenser turned back once more to Ireland, to his clerk-
ship of the Council of Munster, which he soon resigned ;
to be worried with law-suits about "lands in Shanbally-
more and Ballingrath," by his time-serving and oppressive
Irish neighbour, Maurice Roche, Lord Fermoy ; to brood
still over his lost ideal and hero, Sidney ; to write the
story of his visit in the pastoral supplement to the *Shepherd's Calendar*, *Colin Clout's come home again* ; to
pursue the story of Gloriana's knights ; and to find among
the Irish maidens another Elizabeth, a wife instead of a
queen, whose wooing and winning were to give new
themes to his imagination.

CHAPTER V.

THE FAERY QUEEN.

" *Uncouth* [=unknown], *unkist*," are the words from Chaucer,[1] with which the friend, who introduced Spenser's earliest poetry to the world, bespeaks forbearance, and promises matter for admiration and delight in the *Shepherd's Calendar*. " You have to know my new poet, he says in effect : and when you have learned his ways, you will find how much you have to honour and love him." " I doubt not," he says, with a boldness of prediction, manifestly sincere, which is remarkable about an unknown man, " that so soon as his name shall come into the knowledge of men, and his worthiness be sounded in the trump of fame, but that he shall be not only kissed, but also beloved of all, embraced of the most, and wondered at of the best." Never was prophecy more rapidly and more signally verified, probably beyond the prophet's largest expectation. But he goes on to explain and indeed apologize for certain features of the new poet's work, which even to readers of that day might seem open to exception. And to readers of to-day, the phrase, *uncouth, unkist*, certainly expresses what many have to confess, if they are honest, as to their first acquaintance with the

---

[1] " Unknow, unkyst ; and lost, that is unsoght."
Troylus and Cryseide, lib. i.

Faery Queen. Its place in literature is established beyond
controversy. Yet its first and unfamiliar aspect inspires
respect, perhaps interest, rather than attracts and satisfies.
It is not the remoteness of the subject alone, nor the
distance of three centuries which raises a bar between it
and those to whom it is new. Shakespere becomes familiar
to us from the first moment. The impossible legends of
Arthur have been made in the language of to-day once
more to touch our sympathies, and have lent themselves
to express our thoughts. But at first acquaintance the
Faery Queen to many of us has been disappointing. It
has seemed not only antique, but artificial. It has
seemed fantastic. It has seemed, we cannot help avowing,
tiresome. It is not till the early appearances have worn
off, and we have learned to make many allowances and to
surrender ourselves to the feelings and the standards by
which it claims to affect and govern us, that we really
find under what noble guidance we are proceeding, and
what subtle and varied spells are ever round us.

I. The *Faery Queen* is the work of an unformed literature, the product of an unperfected art. English poetry,
English language, in Spenser's, nay in Shakespere's day,
had much to learn, much to unlearn. They never, perhaps, have been stronger or richer, than in that marvellous
burst of youth, with all its freedom of invention, of
observation, of reflection. But they had not that which
only the experience and practice of eventful centuries
could give them. Even genius must wait for the gifts
of time. It cannot forerun the limitations of its day,
nor anticipate the conquests and common possessions of
the future. Things are impossible to the first great
masters of art which are easy to their second-rate suc-
cessors. The possibility, or the necessity of breaking

through some convention, of attempting some unattempted effort, had not, among other great enterprises, occurred to them. They were laying the steps in a magnificent fashion on which those after them were to rise. But we ought not to shut our eyes to mistakes or faults to which attention had not yet been awakened, or for avoiding which no reasonable means had been found. To learn from genius, we must try to recognize, both what is still imperfect, and what is grandly and unwontedly successful. There is no great work of art, not excepting even the Iliad or the Parthenon, which is not open, especially in point of ornament, to the scoff of the scoffer, or to the injustice of those who do not mind being unjust. But all art belongs to man; and man, even when he is greatest, is always limited and imperfect.

The *Faery Queen*, as a whole, bears on its face a great fault of construction. It carries with it no adequate account of its own story; it does not explain itself, or contain in its own structure what would enable a reader to understand how it arose. It has to be accounted for by a prose explanation and key outside of itself. The poet intended to reserve the central event, which was the occasion of all the adventures of the poem, till they had all been related, leaving them as it were in the air, till at the end of twelve long books the reader should at last be told how the whole thing had originated, and what it was all about. He made the mistake of confounding the answer to a riddle with the crisis which unties the tangle of a plot and satisfies the suspended interest of a tale. None of the great model poems before him, however full of digression and episode, had failed to arrange their story with clearness. They needed no commentary outside themselves to say why they began as they did, and out of

what antecedents they arose. If they started at once
from the middle of things, they made their story, as it unfolded itself, explain, by more or less skilful devices, all
that needed to be known about their beginnings. They
did not think of rules of art. They did of themselves
naturally what a good story-teller does, to make himself
intelligible and interesting ; and it is not easy to be interesting, unless the parts of the story are in their place.

The defect seems to have come upon Spenser when it
was too late to remedy it in the construction of his poem ;
and he adopted the somewhat clumsy expedient of
telling us what the poem itself ought to have told us of
its general story, in a letter to Sir Walter Ralegh. Ralegh
himself, indeed, suggested the letter : apparently (from the
date, Jan. 23, 1590), after the first part had gone through
the press. And without this after-thought, as the twelfth
book was never reached, we should have been left to
gather the outline and plan of the story, from imperfect
glimpses and allusions, as we have to fill up from hints
and assumptions the gaps of an unskilful narrator, who
leaves out what is essential to the understanding of his
tale.

Incidentally, however, this letter is an advantage : for
we have in it the poet's own statement of his purpose in
writing, as well as a necessary sketch of his story. His
allegory, as he had explained to Bryskett and his friends,
had a moral purpose. He meant to shadow forth, under
the figures of twelve knights, and in their various exploits,
the characteristics of "a gentleman or noble person,"
"fashioned in virtuous and gentle discipline." He took
his machinery from the popular legends about King Arthur,
and his heads of moral philosophy from the current Aris-
totelian catalogue of the Schools.

Sir, knowing how doubtfully all Allegories may be construed, and this booke of mine, which I have entituled the Faery Queene, being a continued Allegory, or darke conceit, I haue thought good, as well for avoyding of gealous opinions and misconstructions, as also for your better light in reading thereof, (being so by you commanded,) to discover unto you the general intention and meaning, which in the whole course thereof I have fashioned, without expressing of any particular purposes, or by accidents, therein occasioned. The generall end therefore of all the booke is to fashion a gentleman or noble person in vertuous and gentle discipline: Which for that I conceived shoulde be most plausible and pleasing, being coloured with an historicall fiction, the which the most part of men delight to read, rather for variety of matter then for profite of the ensample, I chose the historye of King Arthure, as most fittte for the excellency of his person, being made famous by many mens former workes, and also furthest from the daunger of envy, and suspition of present time. In which I have followed all the antique Poets historicall; first Homere, who in the Persons of Agamemnon and Ulysses hath ensampled a good governour and a vertuous man, the one in his Ilias, the other in his Odysseis: then Virgil, whose like intention was to doe in the person of Aeneas: after him Ariosto comprised them both in his Orlando: and lately Tasso dissevered them againe, and formed both parts in two persons, namely that part which they in Philosophy call Ethice, or vertues of a private man, coloured in his Rinaldo; the other named Politice in his God-fredo. By ensample of which excellente Poets, I labour to pourtraict in Arthure, before he was king, the image of a brave knight, perfected in the twelve private morall vertues, as Aris-totle hath devised; the which is the purpose of these first twelve bookes: which if I finde to be well accepted, I may be perhaps encoraged to frame the other part of polliticke vertues in his person, after that hee came to be king.

Then, after explaining that he meant the *Faery Queen* "for glory in general intention, but in particular" for Elizabeth, and his Faery Land for her kingdom, he proceeds to explain, what the first three books hardly explain, what the Faery Queen had to do with the structure of the poem.

But, because the beginning of the whole worke seemeth abrupte, and as depending upon other antecedents, it needs that ye know the occasion of these three knights seuerall adventures. For the Methode of a Poet historical is not such, as of an Historiographer. For an Historiographer discourseth of affayres orderly as they were donne, accounting as well the times as the actions; but a Poet thrusteth into the middest, even where it most concerneth him, and there recoursing to the thinges forepaste, and divining of thinges to come, maketh a pleasing Analysis of all.

The beginning therefore of my history, if it were to be told by an Historiographer should be the twelfth booke, which is the last; where I devise that the Faery Queene kept her Annuall feaste xii. dayes; uppon which xii. severall dayes, the occasions of the xii. severall adventures hapned, which, being undertaken by xii. severall knights, are in these xii. books severally handled and discoursed. The first was this. In the beginning of the feast, there presented him selfe a tall clownishe younge man, who falling before the Queene of Faries desired a boone (as the manner then was) which during that feast she might not refuse; which was that hee might have the atchievement of any adventure, which during that feaste should happen: that being graunted, he rested him on the floore, unfitte through his rusticity for a better place. Soone after entred a faire Ladye in mourning weedes, riding on a white Asse, with a dwarfe behinde her leading a warlike steed, that bore the Armes of a knight, and his speare in the dwarfes hand. Shee, falling before the Queene of Faeries, complayned that her father and mother, an ancient King and Queene, had beene by an huge dragon many years shut up in a brasen Castle, who thence suffred them not to yssew; and therefore besought the Faery Queene to assygne her some one of her knights to take on him that exployt. Presently that clownish person, upstarting, desired that adventure: whereat the Queene much wondering,

and the Lady much gainesaying, yet he earnestly importuned
his desire. In the end the Lady told him, that unlesse that
armour which she brought would serve him (that is, the
armour of a Christian man specified by Saint Paul, vi. Ephes.)
that he could not succeed in that enterprise; which being forthwith put upon him, with dewe furnitures thereunto, he seemed
the goodliest man in al that company, and was well liked of the
Lady. And eftesoones taking on him knighthood, and mounting on that straunge courser, he went forth with her on that
adventure: where beginneth the first booke, viz.

A gentle knight was pricking on the playne, &c.

That it was not without reason that this explanatory key was
prefixed to the work, and that either Spenser or Ralegh
felt it to be almost indispensable, appear from the con-
cluding paragraph.

Thus much, Sir, I have briefly overronne to direct your
understanding to the wel-head of the History; that from thence
gathering the whole intention of the conceit, ye may as in a
handfull gripe al the discourse, which otherwise may happily
seeme tedious and confused.

According to the plan thus sketched out, we have but a
fragment of the work. It was published in two parcels,
each of three books, in 1590 and 1596 ; and after his death
two cantos, with two stray stanzas, of a seventh book were
found and printed. Each perfect book consists of twelve
cantos of from thirty-five to sixty of his nine-line stanzas.
The books published in 1590 contain, as he states in his
prefatory letter, the legends of *Holiness*, of *Temperance*, and
of *Chastity*. Those published in 1596, contain the legends
of *Friendship*, of *Justice*, and of *Courtesy*. The posthu-
mous cantos are entitled, *Of Mutability*, and are said to
be apparently parcel of a legend of *Constancy*. The poem
which was to treat of the "politic" virtues was never

approached.   Thus we have but a fourth part of the whole
of the projected work.   It is very doubtful whether the
remaining six books were completed.   But it is probable
that a portion of them was written, which, except the
cantos *On Mutability*, has perished.   And the intended
titles or legends of the later books have not been preserved.

Thus the poem was to be an allegorical story ; a story
branching out into twelve separate stories, which themselves would branch out again and involve endless other
stories.   It is a complex scheme to keep well in hand,
and Spenser's art in doing so has been praised by some of
his critics.   But the art, if there is any, is so subtle that
it fails to save the reader from perplexity.   The truth is
that the power of ordering and connecting a long and
complicated plan was not one of Spenser's gifts.   In the
first two books, the allegorical story proceeds from point
to point with fair coherence and consecutiveness.   After
them the attempt to hold the scheme together, except in the
loosest and most general way, is given up as too troublesome or too confined.   The poet prefixes indeed the name
of a particular virtue to each book, but, with slender reference to it, he surrenders himself freely to his abundant flow of ideas, and to whatever fancy or invention
tempts him, and ranges unrestrained over the whole field
of knowledge and imagination.   In the first two books,
the allegory is transparent and the story connected.   The
allegory is of the nature of the *Pilgrim's Progress*.   It
starts from the belief that religion, purified from falsehood, superstition, and sin, is the foundation of all nobleness in man ; and it portrays, under images and with
names, for the most part easily understood, and easily ap-
plied to real counterparts, the struggle which every one at
that time supposed to be going on, between absolute truth

and righteousness on one side, and fatal error and bottomless wickedness on the other. Una, the Truth, the one and only Bride of man's spirit, marked out by the tokens of humility and innocence, and by her power over wild and untamed natures—the single Truth, in contrast to the counterfeit Duessa, false religion, and its actual embodiment in the false rival Queen of Scots—Truth, the object of passionate homage, real with many, professed with all, which after the impostures and scandals of the preceding age, had now become characteristic of that of Elizabeth—Truth, its claims, its dangers, and its champions, are the subject of the first book : and it is represented as leading the manhood of England, in spite, not only of terrible conflict, but of defeat and falls, through the discipline of repentance, to holiness and the blessedness which comes with it. The Red Cross Knight, St. George of England, whose name Georgos, the Ploughman, is dwelt upon, apparently to suggest that from the commonalty, the "tall clownish young men," were raised up the great champions of the Truth,—though sorely troubled by the wiles of Duessa, by the craft of the arch-sorcerer, by the force and pride of the great powers of the Apocalyptic Beast and Dragon, finally overcomes them, and wins the deliverance of Una and her love.

The second book, *Of Temperance*, pursues the subject, and represents the internal conquests of self-mastery, the conquests of a man over his passions, his violence, his covetousness, his ambition, his despair, his sensuality. Sir Guyon, after conquering many foes of goodness, is the destroyer of the most perilous of them all, Acrasia, licentiousness, and her ensnaring Bower of Bliss. But after this, the thread at once of story and allegory, slender henceforth at the best, is neglected and often entirely

lost. The third book, the *Legend of Chastity*, is a
repetition of the ideas of the latter part of the second,
with a heroine, Britomart, in place of the Knight of
the previous book, Sir Guyon, and with a special
glorification of the high-flown and romantic sentiments
about purity, which were the poetic creed of the courtiers of Elizabeth, in flagrant and sometimes in tragic
contrast to their practical conduct of life. The loose
and ill-compacted nature of the plan becomes still more
evident in the second instalment of the work. Even the
special note of each particular virtue becomes more faint
and indistinct. The one law to which the poet feels bound
is to have twelve cantos in each book ; and to do this he
is sometimes driven to what in later times has been
called padding. One of the cantos of the third book
is a genealogy of British kings from Geoffrey of Mon-
mouth ; one of the cantos of the *Legend of Friendship* is
made up of an episode, describing the marriage of the
Thames and the Medway, with an elaborate catalogue of
the English and Irish rivers, and the names of the sea-
nymphs. In truth, he had exhausted his proper allegory,
or he got tired of it. His poem became an elastic framework, into which he could fit whatever interested him and
tempted him to composition. The gravity of the first
books disappears. He passes into satire and caricature.
We meet with Braggadochio and Trompart, with the discomfiture of Malecasta, with the conjugal troubles of
Malbecco and Helenore, with the imitation from Ariosto
of the Squire of Dames. He puts into verse a poetical
physiology of the human body ; he translates Lucretius,
and speculates on the origin of human souls ; he speculates, too, on social justice, and composes an argumentative
refutation of the Anabaptist theories of right and equality

among men. As the poem proceeds, he seems to feel
himself more free to introduce what he pleases. Allusions
to real men and events are sometimes clear, at other times
evident, though they have now ceased to be intelligible
to us. His disgust and resentment breaks out at the ways
of the Court in sarcastic moralizing, or in pictures of dark
and repulsive imagery. The characters and pictures of
his friends furnish material for his poem; he does not
mind touching on the misadventures of Ralegh, and
even of Lord Grey, with sly humour or a word of
candid advice. He becomes bolder in the distinct
introduction of contemporary history. The defeat of
Duessa was only figuratively shown in the first portion;
in the second the subject is resumed. As Elizabeth is the
" one form of many names," Gloriana, Belphœbe, Britomart, Mercilla, so " under feigned colours shading a true
case " he deals with her rival. Mary seems at one
time the false Florimel, the creature of enchantment,
stirring up strife, and fought for by the foolish knights
whom she deceives, Blandamour and Paridell, the counterparts of Norfolk and the intriguers of 1571. At another,
she is the fierce Amazonian queen, Radegund, by whom
for a moment, even Arthegal is brought into disgraceful
thraldom, till Britomart, whom he has once fought against,
delivers him. And finally the fate of the typical Duessa
is that of the real Mary Queen of Scots described in great
detail—a liberty in dealing with great affairs of state for
which James of Scotland actually desired that he should
be tried and punished.[2]   So Philip II. is at one time the
Soldan, at another the Spanish monster Geryoneo, at
another the fosterer of Catholic intrigues in France and
Ireland, Grantorto. But real names are also introduced

[2] Hales' *Life*, Globe Edition.

with scarcely any disguise: Guizor, and Burbon, the
Knight who throws away his shield, Henry IV., and his
Lady Flourdelis, the Lady Belge, and her seventeen
sons: the Lady Irena, whom Arthegal delivers. The
overthrow of the Armada, the English war in the
Low Countries, the apostasy of Henry IV., the
deliverance of Ireland from the "great wrong" of
Desmond's rebellion, the giant Grantorto, form, under
more or less transparent allegory, great part of the
Legend of Justice. Nay, Spenser's long fostered revenge
on the lady who had once scorned him, the *Rosalind* of
the *Shepherd's Calendar*, the *Mirabella* of the *Faery
Queen*, and his own late and happy marriage in Ireland,
are also brought in to supply materials for the *Legend of
Courtesy.* So multifarious is the poem, full of all that he
thought, or observed, or felt; a receptacle, without much
care to avoid repetition, or to prune, correct, and condense,
for all the abundance of his ideas, as they welled forth
in his mind day by day. It is really a collection of
separate tales and allegories, as much as the *Arabian
Nights*, or, as its counterpart and rival of our own
century, the *Idylls of the King.* As a whole it is con
fusing: but we need not treat it as a whole. Its continued
interest soon breaks down. But it is probably best that
Spenser gave his mind the vague freedom which suited
it, and that he did not make efforts to tie himself down
to his pre-arranged but too ambitious plan. We can
hardly lose our way in it, for there is no way to lose.
It is a wilderness in which we are left to wander. But
there may be interest and pleasure in a wilderness, if we
are prepared for the wandering.

Still, the complexity, or rather, the uncared-for and
clumsy arrangement of the poem is matter which dis-

turbs a reader's satisfaction, till he gets accustomed to
the poet's way, and resigns himself to it. It is a heroic
poem, in which the heroine, who gives her name to it,
never appears : a story, of which the basis and starting-
point is whimsically withheld for disclosure in the last
book, which was never written. If Ariosto's jumps
and transitions are more audacious, Spenser's intricacy
is more puzzling. Adventures begin which have no
finish. Actors in them drop from the clouds, claim an
interest, and we ask in vain what has become of them.
A vein of what are manifestly contemporary allusions breaks
across the moral drift of the allegory, with an apparently
distinct yet obscured meaning, and one of which it is
the work of dissertations to find the key. The passion of
the age was for ingenious riddling in morality as in love.
And in Spenser's allegories we are not seldom at a loss
to make out what and how much was really intended,
amid a maze of overstrained analogies and over-subtle
conceits, and attempts to hinder a too close and dangerous identification.

Indeed Spenser's mode of allegory, which was historical
as well as moral, and contains a good deal of history, if we
knew it, often seems devised to throw curious readers off
the scent. It was purposely baffling and hazy. A characteristic trait was singled out. A name was transposed
in anagram, like Irena, or distorted, as if by imperfect
pronunciation, like Burbon and Arthegal, or invented to
express a quality, like Una, or Gloriana, or Corceca, or Fra-
dubio, or adopted with no particular reason from the
Morte d'Arthur, or any other old literature. The personage is introduced with some feature, or amid circumstances which seem for a moment to fix the meaning.
But when we look to the sequence of history being kept

up in the sequence of the story, we find ourselves thrown out. A character which fits one person puts on the marks of another : a likeness which we identify with one real person passes into the likeness of some one else. The real, in person, incident, institution, shades off into the ideal; after showing itself by plain tokens, it turns aside out of its actual path of fact, and ends, as the poet thinks it ought to end, in victory or defeat, glory or failure. Prince Arthur passes from Leicester to Sidney, and then back again to Leicester. There are double or treble allegories; Elizabeth is Gloriana, Belphœbe, Britomart, Mercilla, perhaps Amoret ; her rival is Duessa, the false Florimel, probably the fierce temptress, the Amazon Radegund. Thus, what for a moment was clear and definite, fades like the changing fringe of a dispersing cloud. The character which we identified disappears in other scenes and adventures, where we lose sight of all that identified it. A complete transformation destroys the likeness which was begun. There is an intentional dislocation of the parts of the story, when they might make it imprudently close in its reflection of facts or resemblance in portraiture. A feature is shown, a manifest allusion made, and then the poet starts off in other directions, to confuse and perplex all attempts at interpretation, which might be too particular and too certain. This was no doubt merely according to the fashion of the time, and the habits of mind into which the poet had grown. But there were often reasons for it, in an age so suspicious, and so dangerous to those who meddled with high matters of state.

2. Another feature which is on the surface of the *Faery Queen*, and which will displease a reader who has been trained to value what is natural and genuine, is its affec-

tation of the language and the customs of life belonging to
an age which is not its own. It is indeed redolent of the
present : but it is almost avowedly an imitation of what
was current in the days of Chaucer : of what were supposed to be the words, and the social ideas and conditions,
of the age of chivalry. He looked back to the fashions
and ideas of the Middle Ages, as Pindar sought his materials in the legends and customs of the Homeric times,
and created a revival of the spirit of the age of the
Heroes in an age of tyrants and incipient democracies.[3]
The age of chivalry, in Spenser's day far distant, had
yet left two survivals, one real, the other formal. The
real survival was the spirit of armed adventure, which
was never stronger or more stirring than in the gallants
and discoverers of Elizabeth's reign, the captains of the
English companies in the Low Countries, the audacious
sailors who explored unknown oceans and plundered the
Spaniards, the scholars and gentlemen equally ready for
work on sea and land, like Ralegh and Sir Richard
Grenville, of the " Revenge." The formal survival was
the fashion of keeping up the trappings of knightly times,
as we keep up Judge's wigs, court dresses, and Lord
Mayor's shows. In actual life it was seen in pageants
and ceremonies, in the yet lingering parade of jousts and
tournaments, in the knightly accoutrements still worn in
the days of the bullet and the cannon-ball. In the
apparatus of the poet, as all were shepherds, when he
wanted to represent the life of peace and letters, so all
were knights or the foes and victims of knights, when his
theme was action and enterprise. It was the custom that
the Muse masked, to use Spenser's word, under these

---

[3] *Vid.* Keble, *Prælect. Acad.*, xxiv. p. 479, 480.

disguises; and this conventional masquerade of pastoral poetry or knight errantry was the form under which the poetical school that preceded the dramatists naturally expressed their ideas. It seems to us odd that peaceful sheepcotes and love-sick swains should stand for the world of the Tudors and Guises, or that its cunning state-craft and relentless cruelty should be represented by the generous follies of an imaginary chivalry. But it was the fashion which Spenser found, and he accepted it. His genius was not of that sort which breaks out from trammels, but of that which makes the best of what it finds. And whatever we may think of the fashion, at least he gave it new interest and splendour by the spirit with which he threw himself into it.

The condition which he took as the groundwork of his poetical fabric suggested the character of his language. Chaucer was then the " God of English poetry ;" his was the one name which filled a place apart in the history of English verse. Spenser was a student of Chaucer, and borrowed as he judged fit, not only from his vocabulary, but from his grammatical precedents and analogies, with the object of giving an appropriate colouring to what was to be raised as far as possible above familiar life. Besides this, the language was still in such an unsettled state that from a man with resources like Spenser's, it naturally invited attempts to enrich and colour it, to increase its flexibility and power. The liberty of reviving old forms, of adopting from the language of the street and market homely but expressive words or combinations, of following in the track of convenient constructions, of venturing on new and bold phrases, was rightly greater in his time than at a later stage of the language. Many of his words, either invented or preserved, are happy additions; some

which have not taken root in the language, we may
regret. But it was a liberty which he abused. He was
extravagant and unrestrained in his experiments on language. And they were made not merely to preserve or to
invent a good expression. On his own authority, he cuts
down, or he alters a word, or he adopts a mere corrupt
pronunciation, to suit a place in his metre, or because he
wants a rime. Precedents, as Mr. Guest has said, may
no doubt be found for each one of these sacrifices to the
necessities of metre or rime, in some one or other living
dialectic usage, or even in printed books—"*blend*" for
"*blind*," "*misleeke*" for "*mislike*," "*kest*" for "*cast*,"
"*cherry*" for "*cherish*," "*vilde*" for "*vile*," or even
"*wawes*" for "*waves*," because it has to rime to "*jaws*."
But when they are profusely used as they are in Spenser,
they argue, as critics of his own age such as Puttenham,
remarked,—either want of trouble, or want of resource.
In his impatience he is reckless in making a word which
he wants—"fortunize," "mercified," "unblindfold," "re-
live"—he is reckless in making one word do the duty of
another, interchanging actives and passives, transferring
epithets from their proper subjects. The "humbled
grass," is the grass on which a man lies humbled: the
"lamentable eye," is the eye which laments. " His treatment of words," says Mr. Craik, " on such occasions "—
occasions of difficulty to his verse—" is like nothing that
ever was seen, unless it might be Hercules breaking the
back of the Nemean lion. He gives them any sense
and any shape that the case may demand. Sometimes
he merely alters a letter or two ; sometimes he twists
off the head or the tail of the unfortunate vocable
altogether. But this fearless, lordly, truly royal style
makes one only feel the more how easily, if he chose,

he could avoid the necessity of having recourse to such outrages."

His own generation felt his licence to be extreme. "In affecting the ancients," said Ben Jonson, "he writ no language." Daniel writes sarcastically, soon after the *Faery Queen* appeared, of those who

> Sing of knights and Palladines,
> In aged accents and untimely words.

And to us, though students of the language must always find interest in the storehouse of ancient or invented language to be found in Spenser, this mixture of what is obsolete or capriciously new is a bar, and not an unreasonable one, to a frank welcome at first acquaintance. Fuller remarks with some slyness, that "the many Chaucerisms used (for I will not say, affected) by him, are thought by the ignorant to be blemishes, known by the learned to be beauties, in his book; which notwithstanding had been more saleable, if more conformed to our modern language." The grotesque, though it has its place as one of the instruments of poetical effect, is a dangerous element to handle. Spenser's age was very insensible to the presence and the dangers of the grotesque, and he was not before his time in feeling what was unpleasing in incongruous mixtures. Strong in the abundant but unsifted learning of his day, a style of learning, which in his case was strangely inaccurate, he not only mixed the past with the present, fairyland with politics, mythology with the most serious Christian ideas, but he often mixed together the very features which are most discordant, in the colours, forms, and methods by which he sought to produce the effect of his pictures.

3. Another source of annoyance and disappointment is

found in the imperfections and inconsistencies of the poet's
standard of what is becoming to say and to write about.
Exaggeration, diffuseness, prolixity, were the literary
diseases of the age ; an age of great excitement and hope,
which had suddenly discovered its wealth and its powers,
but not the rules of true economy in using them. With
the classics open before it, and alive to much of the grandeur of their teaching, it was almost blind to the spirit of
self-restraint, proportion, and simplicity which governed
the great models. It was left to a later age to discern
these and appreciate them. This unresisted proneness to
exaggeration produced the extravagance and the horrors of
the Elizabethan Drama, full, as it was, nevertheless, of
insight and originality. It only too naturally led the
earlier Spenser astray. What Dryden, in one of his interesting critical prefaces says of himself, is true of Spenser ;
" Thoughts, such as they are, come crowding in so fast
upon me, that my only difficulty is to choose or to reject ;
to run them into verse, or to give them the other harmony
of prose." There was in Spenser a facility for turning
to account all material, original or borrowed, an inconti-
nence of the descriptive faculty, which was ever ready to
exercise itself on any object, the most unfitting and loathsome, as on the noblest, the purest, or the most beautiful.
There are pictures in him which seem meant to turn our
stomach. Worse than that there are pictures which for a
time rank the poet of *Holiness* or *Temperance*, with the
painters who used their great art to represent at once the
most sacred and holiest forms, and also scenes which few
people now like to look upon in company—scenes and
descriptions which may perhaps from the habits of the
time may have been playfully and innocently produced,
but which it is certainly not easy to dwell upon innocently

now. And apart from these serious faults, there is continually haunting us, amid incontestable richness, vigour, and beauty, a sense that the work is over-done. Spenser certainly did not want for humour and an eye for the ridiculous. There is no want in him, either, of that power of epigrammatic terseness, which, in spite of its diffuseness, his age valued and cultivated. But when he gets on a story or a scene, he never knows where to stop. His duels go on stanza after stanza till there is no sound part left in either champion. His palaces, landscapes, pageants, feasts, are taken to pieces in all their parts, and all these parts are likened to some other things. "His abundance," says Mr. Craik, "is often oppressive; *it is like wading among unmown grass.*" And he drowns us in words. His abundant and incongruous adjectives may sometimes, perhaps, startle us unfairly, because their associations and suggestions have quite altered; but very often they are the idle outpouring of an unrestrained affluence of language. The impression remains that he wants a due perception of the absurd, the unnatural, the unnecessary; that he does not care if he makes us smile, or does not know how to help it, when he tries to make us admire or sympathize.

Under this head comes a feature which the "charity of history" may lead us to treat as simple exaggeration, but which often suggests something less pardonable, in the great characters, political or literary, of Elizabeth's reign. This was the gross, shameless, lying flattery paid to the Queen. There is really nothing like it in history. It is unique as a phenomenon that proud, able, free-spoken men, with all their high instincts of what was noble and true, with all their admiration of the Queen's high qualities, should have offered it, even as an unmeaning custom; and that a proud and free-spoken people should not, in the

very genuineness of their pride in her and their loyalty,
have received it with shouts of derision and disgust. The
flattery of Roman emperors and Roman Popes, if as extravagant, was not so personal. Even Louis XIV. was not
celebrated in his dreary old age, as a model of ideal beauty
and a paragon of romantic perfection. It was no worship
of a secluded and distant object of loyalty : the men who
thus flattered knew perfectly well, often by painful experience, what Elizabeth was : able, indeed, high-spirited,
successful, but ungrateful to her servants, capricious, vain,
ill-tempered, unjust, and in her old age, ugly. And yet
the Gloriana of the *Faery Queen*, the Empress of all
nobleness,—Belphœbe, the Princess of all sweetness and
beauty,—Britomart, the armed votaress of all purity,—
Mercilla, the lady of all compassion and grace,—were but
the reflections of the language in which it was then
agreed upon by some of the greatest of Englishmen to
speak, and to be supposed to think, of the Queen.

II. But when all these faults have been admitted, faults
of design and faults of execution—and when it is admitted,
further, that there is a general want of reality, substance,
distinctness, and strength in the personages of the poem
—that, compared with the contemporary drama, Spenser's
knights and ladies and villains are thin and ghostlike,
and that, as Daniel says, he

> Paints shadows in imaginary lines—

it yet remains that our greatest poets since his day have
loved him and delighted in him. He had Shakespere's
praise. Cowley was made a poet by reading him. Dryden
calls Milton " the poetical son of Spenser :" " Milton," he
writes, " has acknowledged to me that Spenser was his
original." Dryden's own homage to him is frequent and

generous. Pope found as much pleasure in the *Faery Queen* in his later years as he had found in reading it when he was twelve years old : and what Milton, Dryden, and Pope admired, Wordsworth too found full of nobleness, purity, and sweetness. What is it that gives the *Faery Queen* its hold on those who appreciate the richness and music of English language, and who in temper and moral standard are quick to respond to English manliness and tenderness? The spell is to be found mainly in three things—(1) in the quaint stateliness of Spenser's imaginary world and its representatives ; (2) in the beauty and melody of his numbers, the abundance and grace of his poetic ornaments, in the recurring and haunting rhythm of numberless passages, in which thought and imagery and language and melody are interwoven in one perfect and satisfying harmony ; and (3) in the intrinsic nobleness of his general aim, his conception of human life, at once so exacting and so indulgent, his high ethical principles and ideals, his unfeigned honour for all that is pure and brave and unselfish and tender, his generous estimate of what is due from man to man of service, affection, and fidelity. His fictions embodied truths of character which with all their shadowy incompleteness were too real and too beautiful to lose their charm with time.

1. Spenser accepted from his age the quaint stateliness which is characteristic of his poem. His poetry is not simple and direct like that of the Greeks. It has not the exquisite finish and felicity of the best of the Latins. It has not the massive grandeur, the depth, the freedom, the shades and subtle complexities of feeling and motive, which the English dramatists found by going straight to nature. It has the stateliness of highly artificial conditions of society, of the Court, the pageant, the tourna-

ment, as opposed to the majesty of the great events in
human life and history, its real vicissitudes, its cata-
strophes, its tragedies, its revolutions, its sins. Throughout the prolonged crisis of Elizabeth's reign, her gay and
dashing courtiers, and even her serious masters of affairs,
persisted in pretending to look on the world in which they
lived, as if through the side scenes of a masque, and relieved against the background of a stage-curtain. Human
life, in those days, counted for little ; fortune, honour,
national existence hung in the balance ; the game was
one in which the heads of kings and queens and great
statesmen were the stakes,—yet the players could not get
out of their stiff and constrained costume, out of their
artificial and fantastic figments of thought, out of their
conceits and affectations of language. They carried it,
with all their sagacity, with all their intensity of purpose,
to the council-board, and the judgment-seat. They carried
it to the scaffold. The conventional supposition was that
at the Court, though every one knew better, all was
perpetual sunshine, perpetual holiday, perpetual triumph,
perpetual love-making. It was the happy reign of the
good and wise and lovely. It was the discomfiture of the
base, the faithless, the wicked, the traitors. This is what
is reflected in Spenser's poem ; at once, its stateliness, for
there was no want of grandeur and magnificence in the
public scene ever before Spenser's imagination ; and its
quaintness, because the whole outward apparatus of
representation was borrowed from what was past, or from
what did not exist, and implied surrounding circumstances
in ludicrous contrast with fact, and men taught themselves
to speak in character, and prided themselves on keeping
it up by substituting for the ordinary language of life and
emotion a cumbrous and involved indirectness of speech.

And yet that quaint stateliness is not without its attractions. We have indeed to fit ourselves for it. But when we have submitted to its demands on our imagination, it carries us along as much as the fictions of the stage. The splendours of the artificial are not the splendours of the natural; yet the artificial has its splendours, which impress and captivate and repay. The grandeur of Spenser's poem is a grandeur like that of a great spectacle, a great array of the forces of a nation, a great series of military effects, a great ceremonial assemblage of all that is highest and most eminent in a country, a coronation, a royal marriage, a triumph, a funeral. So, though Spenser's knights and ladies do what no men ever could do, and speak what no man ever spoke, the procession rolls forward with a pomp which never forgets itself, and with an inexhaustible succession of circumstance, fantasy, and incident. Nor is it always solemn and high-pitched. Its gravity is relieved from time to time with the ridiculous figure or character, the ludicrous incident, the jests and antics of the buffoon. It has been said that Spenser never smiles. He not only smiles, with amusement or sly irony; he wrote what he must have laughed at as he wrote, and meant us to laugh at. He did not describe with a grave face the terrors and misadventures of the boaster Braggadochio and his Squire, whether or not a caricature of the Duke of Alençon and his "gentleman," the "petit singe," Simier. He did not write with a grave face the Irish row about the false Florimel (IV. 5), —

> Then unto Satyran she was adjudged,
> Who was right glad to gaine so goodly meed :
> But Blandamour thereat full greatly grudged,
> And litle prays'd his labours evill speed,

That for to winne the saddle lost the steed.
Ne lesse thereat did Paridell complaine,
And thought t'appeale from that which was decreed
To single combat with Sir Satyrane :
Thereto him Atè stird, new discord to maintaine.

And eke, with these, full many other Knights
She through her wicked working did incense
Her to demaund and chalenge as their rights,
Deserved for their porils recompense.
Amongst the rest, with boastfull vaine pretense,
Stept Braggadochio forth, and as his thrall
Her claym'd, by him in battell wonne long sens :
Whereto her selfe he did to witnesse call :
Who, being askt, accordingly confessed all.

Thereat exceeding wroth was Satyran ;
And wroth with Satyran was Blandamour ;
And wroth with Blandamour was Erivan ;
And at them both Sir Paridell did loure.
So all together stird up strifull stoure,
And readie were new battell to darraine.
Each one profest to be her paramoure,
And vow'd with speare and shield it to maintaine ;
Ne Judges powre, ne reasons rule, mote them restraine.

Nor the behaviour of the "rascal many" at the sight of
the dead Dragon (I. 12),—

And after all the raskall many ran,
Heaped together in rude rablement,
To see the face of that victorious man,
Whom all admired as from heaven sent,
And gazd upon with gaping wonderment ;
But when they came where that dead Dragon lay,
Stretcht on the ground in monstrous large extent,
The sight with ydle feare did them dismay,
Ne durst approch him nigh to touch, or once assay.

Some feard, and fledd ; some feard, and well it fayned ;
One, that would wiser seeme then all the rest,
Warnd him not touch, for yet perhaps remaynd
Some lingring life within his hollow brest,

Or in his wombe might lurke some hidden nest
Of many Dragonettes, his fruitfull seede :
Another saide, that in his eyes did rest
Yet sparckling fyre, and badd thereof take heed ;
Another said, he saw him move his eyes indeed.

One mother, whenas her foolehardy chyld
Did come too neare, and with his talants play,
Halfe dead through feare, her litle babe revyld,
And to her gossibs gan in counsell say ;
' How can I tell, but that his talants may
Yet scratch my sonne, or rend his tender hand ? '
So diversly them selves in vaine they fray ;
Whiles some more bold to measure him nigh stand,
To prove how many acres he did spred of land.

And his humour is not the less real that it affects serious
argument, in the excuse which he urges for his fairy
tales (II. 1).

Right well I wote, most mighty Soveraine,
That all this famous antique history
Of some th' aboundance of an ydle braine
Will judged be, and painted forgery,
Rather then matter of just memory ;
Sith none that breatheth living aire dees know
Where is that happy land of Faery,
Which I so much doe vaunt, yet no where show,
But vouch antiquities, which no body can know.

But let that man with better sence advize,
That of the world least part to us is red ;
And daily how through hardy enterprize
Many great Regions are discovered,
Which to late age were never mentioned
Who ever heard of th' Indian Peru ?
Or who in venturous vessell measured
The Amazon huge river, now found trew
Or fruitfullest Virginia who did ever vew ?

Yet all these were, when no man did them know,
Yet have from wisest ages hidden beene;
And later times thinges more unknowne shall show.
Why then should witlesse man so much misweene,

That nothing is but that which he hath seene ?
What if within the Moones fayre shining spheare,
What if in every other starre unseene
Of other worldes he happily should heare,
He wonder would much more; yet such to some appeare.

The general effect is almost always lively and rich :
all is buoyant and full of movement. That it is also
odd, that we see strange costumes and hear a language
often formal and obsolete, that we are asked to take for
granted some very unaccustomed supposition and extravagant assumption, does not trouble us more than the usages
and sights, so strange to ordinary civil life, of a camp, or a
royal levée. All is in keeping, whatever may be the
details of the pageant ; they harmonize with the effect of
the whole, like the gargoyles and quaint groups in a
Gothic building harmonize with its general tone of majesty
and subtle beauty ;—nay, as ornaments, in themselves of
bad taste, like much of the ornamentation of the Renaissance styles, yet find a not unpleasing place in compositions grandly and nobly designed :

So discord oft in music makes the sweeter lay.

Indeed, it is curious how much of real variety is got out
of a limited number of elements and situations. The spectacle, though consisting only of knights, ladies, dwarfs,
pagans, " salvage men," enchanters, and monsters, and
other well-worn machinery of the books of chivalry, is
ever new, full of vigour and fresh images, even if, as
sometimes happens, it repeats itself. There is a majestic
unconsciousness of all violations of probability, and of the
strangeness of the combinations which it unrolls before
us.

    2. But there is not only stateliness : there is sweetness

and beauty. Spenser's perception of beauty of all kinds
was singularly and characteristically quick and sympa-
thetic. It was one of his great gifts; perhaps the most
special and unstinted. Except Shakespere, who had it
with other and greater gifts, no one in that time approached to Spenser, in feeling the presence of that com-
manding and mysterious idea, compounded of so many
things, yet of which the true secret escapes us still, to
which we give the name of beauty. A beautiful scene, a
beautiful person, a beautiful poem, a mind and character
with that combination of charms, which, for want of
another word, we call by that half-spiritual, half-material
word "beautiful," at once set his imagination at work to
respond to it and reflect it. His means of reflecting it
were as abundant as his sense of it was keen. They were
only too abundant. They often betrayed him by their
affluence and wonderful readiness to meet his call. Say
what we will, and a great deal may be said, of his lavish
profusion, his heady and uncontrolled excess, in the richness of picture and imagery in which he indulges,—
still there it lies before us, like the most gorgeous of
summer gardens, in the glory and brilliancy of its varied
blooms, in the wonder of its strange forms of life, in the
changefulness of its exquisite and delicious scents. No
one who cares for poetic beauty can be insensible to it.
He may criticize it. He may have too much of it. He
may prefer something more severe and chastened. He
may observe on the waste of wealth and power. He may
blame the prodigal expense of language, and the long
spaces which the poet takes up to produce his effect. He
may often dislike or distrust the moral aspect of the poet's
impartial sensitiveness to all outward beauty,—the im-
partiality which makes him throw all his strength into

L

his pictures of Acrasia's Bower of Bliss, the Garden of
Adonis, and Busirane's Masque of Cupid. But there is
no gainsaying the beauty which never fails and dis-
appoints, open the poem where you will. There is no
gainsaying its variety, often so unexpected and novel.
Face to face with the Epicurean idea of beauty and
pleasure is the counter-charm of purity, truth, and duty.
Many poets have done justice to each one separately.
Few have shown, with such equal power, why it is that
both have their roots in man's divided nature, and struggle,
as it were, for the mastery. Which can be said to be the
most exquisite in all beauty of imagination, of refined
language, of faultless and matchless melody, of these two
passages, in which the same image is used for the most
opposite purposes ;—first, in that song of temptation, the
sweetest note in that description of Acrasia's Bower of
Bliss, which, as a picture of the spells of pleasure, has
never been surpassed ; and next, to represent that stainless
and glorious purity which is the professed object of his
admiration and homage. In both the beauty of the rose
furnishes the theme of the poet's treatment. In the first, it
is the "lovely lay" which meets the knight of Temperance
amid the voluptuousness which he is come to assail and
punish.

The whiles some one did chaunt this lovely lay :
Ah ! see, whoso fayre thing doest faine to see,
In springing flowre the image of thy day.
Ah ! see the Virgin Rose, how sweetly shee
Doth first peepe foorth with bashfull modestee,
That fairer seemes the lesse ye see her may.
Lo ! see soone after how more bold and free
Her bared bosome she doth broad display ;
Lo ! see soone after how she fades and falls away.

So passeth, in the passing of a day,
Of mortall life the leafe, the bud, the flowre ;

No more doth florish after first decay,
That earst was sought to deck both bed and bowre
Of many a lady, and many a Paramowre.
Gather therefore the Rose whilest yet is prime,
For soone comes age that will her pride deflowre;
Gather the Rose of love whilest yet is time,
Whilest loving thou mayst loved be with equall crime.

In the other, it images the power of the will—that power over circumstance and the storms of passion, to command obedience to reason and the moral law, which Milton sung so magnificently in *Comus*:—

That daintie Rose, the daughter of her Morne,
More deare then life she tendered, whose flowre
The girlond of her honour did adorne:
Ne suffred she the Middayes scorching powre,
Ne the sharp Northerne wind thereon to showre;
But lapped up her silken leaves most chayre,
When so the froward skye began to lowre;
But, soone as calmed was the christall ayre,
She did it fayre dispred and let to florish fayre.

Eternall God, in his almightie powre,
To make ensample of his heavenly grace,
In Paradize whylome did plant this flowre;
Whence he it fetcht out of her native place,
And did in stocke of earthly flesh enrace,
That mortall men her glory should admyre.
In gentle Ladies breste, and bounteous race
Of woman kind, it fayrest Flowre doth spyre,
And beareth fruit of honour and all chast desyre.

Fayre ympes of beautie, whose bright shining beames
Adorne the worlde with like to heavenly light,
And to your willes both royalties and Reames
Subdew, through conquest of your wondrous might,
With this fayre flowre your goodly girlonds dight
Of chastity and vertue virginall,
That shall embellish more your beautie bright,
And crowne your heades with heavenly coronall,
Such as the Angels weare before Gods tribunall!

L 2

This sense of beauty, and command of beautiful expression is not seen only in the sweetness of which both
these passages are examples. Its range is wide. Spenser
had in his nature besides sweetness, his full proportion
of the stern and high manliness of his generation; indeed,
he was not without its severity, its hardness, its uncon-
sidering and cruel harshness, its contemptuous indifference
to suffering and misery when on the wrong side. Noble
and heroic ideals captivate him by their attractions. He
kindles naturally and genuinely at what proves and
draws out men's courage, their self-command, their self-
sacrifice. He sympathizes as profoundly with the strangeness of their condition, with the sad surprises in their
history and fate, as he gives himself up with little restraint
to what is charming and even intoxicating in it. He can
moralize with the best in terse and deep-reaching apoph-
thegms of melancholy or even despairing experience. He
can appreciate the mysterious depths and awful outlines
of theology—of what our own age can see nothing in, but
a dry and scholastic dogmatism. His great contemporaries
were, more perhaps than the men of any age, many-sided.
He shared their nature; and he used all that he had of
sensitiveness and of imaginative and creative power, in
bringing out its manifold aspects, and sometimes contradictory feelings and aims. Not that beauty, even varied
beauty, is the uninterrupted attribute of his work. It
alternates with much that no indulgence can call beautiful.
It passes but too easily into what is commonplace, or
forced, or unnatural, or extravagant, or careless and poor,
or really coarse and bad. He was a negligent corrector.
He only at times gave himself the trouble to condense
and concentrate. But for all this, the *Faery Queen* glows
and is ablaze with beauty; and that beauty is so rich, so

real, and so uncommon, that for its sake the severest
readers of Spenser have pardoned much that is discordant
with it, much that in the reading has wasted their time
and disappointed them.

There is one portion of the beauty of the *Faery Queen*,
which in its perfection and fulness had never yet been
reached in English poetry. This was the music and
melody of his verse. It was this wonderful, almost
unfailing sweetness of numbers which probably as much
as anything set the *Faery Queen* at once above all
contemporary poetry. The English language is really a
musical one, and say what people will, the English ear
is very susceptible to the infinite delicacy and suggestiveness of musical rhythm and cadence. Spenser found the
secret of it. The art has had many and consummate
masters since, as different in their melody as in their
thoughts from Spenser. And others at the time, Shakespere pre-eminently, heard, only a little later, the same
grandeur, and the same subtle beauty in the sounds of
their mother-tongue, only waiting the artist's skill to be
combined and harmonized into strains of mysterious
fascination. But Spenser was the first to show that he
had acquired a command over what had hitherto been
heard only in exquisite fragments, passing too soon into
roughness and confusion. It would be too much to say
that his cunning never fails, that his ear is never dull or
off its guard. But when the length and magnitude of
the composition are considered, with the restraints imposed by the new nine-line stanza, however convenient
it may have been, the vigour, the invention, the volume
and rush of language, and the keenness and truth of ear
amid its diversified tasks are indeed admirable, which
could keep up so prolonged and so majestic a stream of

original and varied poetical melody. If his stanzas are
monotonous, it is with the grand monotony of the sea-
shore, where billow follows billow, each swelling diversely,
and broken into different curves and waves upon its
mounting surface, till at last it falls over, and spreads
and rushes up in a last long line of foam upon the beach.

3. But all this is but the outside shell and the fancy
framework in which the substance of the poem is enclosed.
Its substance is the poet's philosophy of life. It shadows
forth, in type and parable, his ideal of the perfection of
the human character, with its special features, its trials,
its achievements. There were two accepted forms in
poetry in which this had been done by poets. One
was under the image of warfare. The other was under
the image of a journey or voyage. Spenser chose the
former, as Dante and Bunyan chose the latter. Spenser
looks on the scene of the world as a continual battle-field.
It was such in fact to his experience in Ireland, testing
the mettle of character, its loyalty, its sincerity, its endurance. His picture of character is by no means painted
with sentimental tenderness. He portrays it in the rough
work of the struggle and the toil, always hardly tested by
trial, often overmatched, deceived, defeated, and even
delivered by its own default to disgrace and captivity.
He had full before his eyes what abounded in the society
of his day, often in its noblest representatives—the
strange perplexing mixture of the purer with the baser
elements, in the high-tempered and aspiring activity of
his time. But it was an ideal of character which had in
it high aims and serious purposes, which was armed with
fortitude and strength, which could recover itself after
failure and defeat.

The unity of a story, or an allegory—that chain and

backbone of continuous interest, implying a progress and
leading up to a climax, which holds together the great
poems of the world, the *Iliad* and *Odyssey*, the *Æneid*,
the *Commedia*, the *Paradise Lost*, the *Jerusalem Deli-*
vered—this is wanting in the *Faery Queen.* The unity
is one of character and its ideal. That character of
the completed man, raised above what is poor and low,
and governed by noble tempers and pure principles, has
in Spenser two conspicuous elements. In the first place,
it is based on manliness. In the personages which illus-
trate the different virtues, Holiness, Justice, Courtesy,
and the rest, the distinction is not in nicely discriminated
features or shades of expression, but in the trials and the
occasions which call forth a particular action or effort :
yet the manliness which is at the foundation of all that
is good in them is a universal quality common to them
all, rooted and imbedded in the governing idea or standard of moral charater in the poem. It is not merely
courage, it is not merely energy, it is not merely strength.
It is the quality of soul which frankly accepts the conditions in human life, of labour, of obedience, of effort, of un-
equal success, which does not quarrel with them or evade
them, but takes for granted with unquestioning alacrity
that man is called—by his call to high aims and destiny
—to a continual struggle with difficulty, with pain, with
evil, and makes it the point of honour not to be dismayed
or wearied out by them. It is a cheerful and serious will-
ingness for hard work and endurance, as being inevitable
and very bearable necessities, together with even a pleasure
in encountering trials which put a man on his mettle, an
enjoyment of the contest and the risk, even in play. It
is the quality which seizes on the paramount idea of
duty, as something which leaves a man no choice ; which

despises and breaks through the inferior considerations
and motives—trouble, uncertainty, doubt, curiosity—
which hang about and impede duty ; which is impatient
with the idleness and childishness of a life of mere amusement, or mere looking on, of continued and self-satisfied
levity, of vacillation, of clever and ingenious trifling. Spenser's manliness is quite consistent with long pauses of rest,
with intervals of change, with great craving for enjoyment
—nay, with great lapses from its ideal, with great mixtures
of selfishness, with coarseness, with licentiousness, with
injustice and inhumanity. It may be fatally diverted
into bad channels ; it may degenerate into a curse and
scourge to the world. But it stands essentially distinct
from the nature which shrinks from difficulty, which is
appalled at effort, which has no thought of making an
impression on things around it, which is content with
passively receiving influences and distinguishing between
emotions, which feels no call to exert itself, because it
recognizes no aim valuable enough to rouse it, and no
obligation strong enough to command it. In the character
of his countrymen round him, in its highest and in its
worst features, in its noble ambition, its daring enterprise,
its self-devotion, as well as in its pride, its intolerance,
its fierce self-will, its arrogant claims of superiority,
moral, political, religious, Spenser saw the example of that
strong and resolute manliness, which, once set on great
things, feared nothing—neither toil nor disaster nor
danger, in their pursuit. Naturally and unconsciously,
he laid it at the bottom of all his portraitures of noble
and virtuous achievement in the *Faery Queen*.

All Spenser's " virtues " spring from a root of manliness. Strength, simplicity of aim, elevation of spirit,
courage are presupposed as their necessary conditions.

But they have with him another condition as universal.
They all grow and are nourished from the soil of
love ; the love of beauty, the love and service of fair
women.   This of course, is a survival from the ages of
chivalry, an inheritance bequeathed from the minstrels of
France, Italy, and Germany to the rising poetry of Europe.
Spenser's types of manhood are imperfect without the
idea of an absorbing and overmastering passion of love ;
without a devotion, as to the principal and most worthy
object of life, to the service of a beautiful lady, and to
winning her affection and grace.   The influence of this
view of life comes out in numberless ways.   Love comes
on the scene in shapes which are exquisitely beautiful,
in all its purity, its tenderness, its unselfishness.   But
the claims of its all-ruling and irresistible might are also
only too readily verified in the passions of men ; in the
follies of love, its entanglements, its mischiefs, its foulness.
In one shape or another it meets us at every turn ; it is
never absent ; it is the motive and stimulant of the whole
activity of the poem.   The picture of life held up before
us is the literal rendering of Coleridge's lines :—

> All thoughts, all passions, all delights,
> Whatever stirs this mortal frame,
> Are all but ministers of Love,
>   And feed his sacred flame.

We still think with Spenser about the paramount place
of manliness, as the foundation of all worth in human
character.   We have ceased to think with him about the
rightful supremacy of love, even in the imaginative conception of human life.   We have ceased to recognize in
it the public claims of almost a religion, which it has in
Spenser.   Love will ever play a great part in human life

to the end of time. It will be an immense element in its
happiness, perhaps a still greater one in its sorrows, its
disasters, its tragedies. It is still an immense power in
shaping and colouring it, both in fiction and reality ; in
the family, in the romance, in the fatalities and the
prosaic ruin of vulgar fact. But the place given to it
by Spenser is to our thoughts and feelings even ludi-
crously extravagant. An enormous change has taken place
in the ideas of society on this point : it is one of the
things which make a wide chasm between centuries and
generations which yet are of " the same passions," and have
in temper, tradition and language, so much in common.
The ages of the Courts of Love, whom Chaucer reflected
and whose ideas passed on through him to Spenser, are
to us simply strange and abnormal states through which
society has passed, to us beyond understanding and almost
belief. The perpetual love-making, as one of the first
duties and necessities of a noble life, the space which it
must fill in the cares and thoughts of all gentle and high-
reaching spirits, the unrestrained language of admiration
and worship, the unrestrained yielding to the impulses,
the anxieties, the pitiable despair and agonies of love,
the subordination to it of all other pursuits and aims,
the weeping and wailing and self-torturing which it
involves, all this is so far apart from what we know of
actual life, the life not merely of work and business, but
the life of affection, and even of passion, that it makes
the picture of which it is so necessary a part, seem to us
in the last degree, unreal, unimaginable, grotesquely
ridiculous. The quaint love sometimes found among
children, so quickly kindled, so superficial, so violent in
its language and absurd in its plans, is transferred with
the utmost gravity to the serious proceedings of the wise

and good. In the highest characters it is chastened,
refined, purified : it appropriates, indeed, language due
only to the divine, it almost simulates idolatry; yet it
belongs to the best part of man's nature. But in the
lower and average characters, it is not so respectable ; it
is apt to pass into mere toying pastime and frivolous love
of pleasure : it astonishes us often by the readiness with
which it displays an affinity for the sensual and impure,
the corrupting and debasing sides of the relations between
the sexes. But however it appears, it is throughout a
very great affair, not merely with certain persons, or
under certain circumstances, but with every one : it
obtrudes itself in public, as the natural and recognized
motive of plans of life and trials of strength ; it is the
great spur of enterprise, and its highest and most glorious
reward. A world of which this is the law, is not even
in fiction a world which we can conceive possible, or with,
which experience enables us to sympathize.

It is, of course, a purely artificial and conventional
reading of the facts of human life and feeling. Such
conventional readings and renderings belong in a measure
to all art ; but in its highest forms they are corrected,
interpreted, supplemented by the presence of interspersed
realities which every one recognizes. But it was one of
Spenser's disadvantages, that two strong influences combined to entangle him in this fantastic and grotesque
way of exhibiting the play and action of the emotions of
love. This all-absorbing, all-embracing passion of love,
at least, this way of talking about it, was the fashion of
the Court. Further, it was the fashion of poetry, which
he inherited ; and he was not the man to break through
the strong bands of custom and authority. In very much
he was an imitator. He took what he found ; what was

his own was his treatment of it. He did not trouble
himself with inconsistencies, or see absurdities and incon-
gruities. Habit and familiar language made it not strange
that in the Court of Elizabeth, the most high-flown sentiments should be in every one's mouth about the sub-
limities and refinements of love, while every one was busy
with keen ambition, and unscrupulous intrigue. The
same blinding power kept him from seeing the monstrous
contrast between the claims of the queen to be the ideal
of womanly purity—claims recognized and echoed in ten
thousand extravagant compliments—and the real licentiousness common all round her among her favourites.
All these strange contradictions, which surprise and shock
us, Spenser assumed as natural. He built up his fictions
on them, as the dramatist built on a basis, which, though
more nearly approaching to real life, yet differed widely
from it in many of its preliminary and collateral suppo-
sitions ; or as the novelist builds up his on a still closer
adherence to facts and experience. In this matter Spenser appears with a kind of double self. At one time he
speaks as one penetrated and inspired by the highest and
purest ideas of love, and filled with aversion and scorn for
the coarser forms of passion—for what is ensnaring and
treacherous, as well as for what is odious and foul. At
another, he puts forth all his power to bring out its most
dangerous and even debasing aspects in highly coloured
pictures, which none could paint without keen sympathy
with what he takes such pains to make vivid and fasci-
nating. The combination is not like anything modern, for
both the elements are in Spenser so unquestionably and
simply genuine. Our modern poets are, with all their
variations in this respect, more homogeneous ; and where
one conception of love and beauty has taken hold of a

man, the other does not easily come in. It is impossible
to imagine Wordsworth dwelling with zest on visions and
imagery, on which Spenser has lavished all his riches.
There can be no doubt of Byron's real habits of thought
and feeling on subjects of this kind, even when his language for the occasion is the chastest; we detect in it the
mood of the moment, perhaps spontaneous, perhaps put
on, but in contradiction to the whole movement of the
man's true nature. But Spenser's words do not ring
hollow. With a kind of unconsciousness and innocence,
which we now find hard to understand, and which perhaps belongs to the early childhood or boyhood of a literature, he passes abruptly from one standard of thought and
feeling to another; and is quite as much in earnest when
he is singing the pure joys of chastened affections, as he is
when he is writing with almost riotous luxuriance what
we are at this day ashamed to read. Tardily, indeed, he
appears to have acknowledged the contradiction. At the
instance of two noble ladies of the Court, he composed
two Hymns of Heavenly Love and Heavenly Beauty,
to "retract" and "reform" two earlier ones composed in
praise of earthly love and beauty. But, characteristically,
he published the two pieces together, side by side in
the same volume.

In the *Faery Queen*, Spenser has brought out, not
the image of the great Gloriana, but in its various aspects,
a form of character which was then just coming on the
stage of the world, and which has played a great part in
it since. As he has told us, he aimed at presenting
before us, in the largest sense of the word, the English
gentleman. It was as a whole a new character in the
world. It had not really existed in the days of feudalism
and chivalry, though features of it had appeared, and its

descent was traced from those times : but they were too
wild and coarse, too turbulent and disorderly, for a character which, however ready for adventure and battle,
looked to peace, refinement, order, and law as the true conditions of its perfection. In the days of Elizabeth it was
beginning to fill a large place in English life. It was
formed amid the increasing cultivation of the nation, the
increasing varieties of public service, the awakening responsibilities to duty and calls to self-command. Still
making much of the prerogative of noble blood and
family honours, it was something independent of nobility
and beyond it. A nobleman might have in him the
making of a gentleman : but it was the man himself of
whom the gentleman was made. Great birth, even great
capacity, were not enough ; there must be added a new
delicacy of conscience, a new appreciation of what is
beautiful and worthy of honour, a new measure of the
strength and nobleness of self-control, of devotion to
unselfish interests. This idea of manhood, based not
only on force and courage, but on truth, on refinement,
on public spirit, on soberness and modesty, on consideration for others, was taking possession of the younger
generation of Elizabeth's middle years. Of course the
idea was very imperfectly apprehended, still more imperfectly realized. But it was something which on the
same scale had not been yet, and which was to be the
seed of something greater. It was to grow into those
strong, simple, noble characters, pure in aim and devoted
to duty, the Falklands, the Hampdens, who amid so
much evil form such a remarkable feature in the Civil
Wars, both on the Royalist and the Parliamentary sides.
It was to grow into that high type of cultivated English
nature, in the present and the last century, common both

to its monarchical and its democratic embodiments, than which, with all its faults and defects, our western civilization has produced few things more admirable.

There were three distinguished men of that time, who one after another were Spenser's friends and patrons, and who were men in whom he saw realized his conceptions of human excellence and nobleness. They were Sir Philip Sidney, Lord Grey of Wilton, and Sir Walter Ralegh : and the *Faery Queen* reflects, as in a variety of separate mirrors and spiritualized forms, the characteristics of these men and of such as they. It reflects their conflicts, their temptations, their weaknesses, the evils they fought with, the superiority with which they towered over meaner and poorer natures. Sir Philip Sidney may be said to have been the first typical example in English society of the true gentleman. The charm which attracted men to him in life, the fame which he left behind him, are not to be accounted for simply by his accomplishments as a courtier, a poet, a lover of literature, a gallant soldier ; above all this there was something not found in the strong or brilliant men about him, a union and harmony of all high qualities differing from any of them separately, which gave a fire of its own to his literary enthusiasm, and a sweetness of its own to his courtesy. Spenser's admiration for that bright but short career was strong and lasting. Sidney was to him a verification of what he aspired to and imagined ; a pledge that he was not dreaming, in portraying Prince Arthur's greatness of soul, the religious chivalry of the Red Cross Knight of Holiness, the manly purity and self-control of Sir Guyon. It is too much to say that in Prince Arthur, the hero of the poem, he always intended Sidney. In the first place, it is clear that under that character Spenser in places pays compli-

ments to Leicester, in whose service he began life, and
whose claims on his homage he ever recognized. Prince
Arthur is certainly Leicester, in the historical passages in
the Fifth Book relating to the war in the Low Countries
in 1576 : and no one can be meant but Leicester in the bold
allusion in the First Book (ix. 17) to Elizabeth's supposed
thoughts of marrying him. In the next place, allegory,
like caricature, is not bound to make the same person and
the same image always or perfectly coincide ; and Spenser
makes full use of this liberty. But when he was painting
the picture of the Kingly Warrior, in whom was to be
summed up in a magnificent unity the diversified graces
of other men, and who was to be ever ready to help and
support his fellows in their hour of need, and in their
conflict with evil, he certainly had before his mind the
well-remembered lineaments of Sidney's high and generous nature. And he further dedicated a separate
book, the last that he completed, to the celebration of
Sidney's special " virtue " of Courtesy. The martial
strain of the poem changes once more to the pastoral
of the *Shepherd's Calendar* to describe Sidney's wooing
of Frances Walsingham, the fair Pastorella ; his conquests by his sweetness and grace over the churlishness
of rivals ; and his triumphant war against the monster
spirit of ignorant and loud-tongued insolence, the " Blatant
Beast " of religious, political, and social slander.

Again, in Lord Grey of Wilton, gentle by nature, but
so stern in the hour of trial, called reluctantly to cope
not only with anarchy, but with intrigue and disloyalty,
finding selfishness and thanklessness everywhere, but
facing all and doing his best with a heavy heart, and
ending his days prematurely under detraction and disgrace, Spenser had before him a less complete character

than Sidney, but yet one of grand and severe manliness, in which were conspicuous a religious hatred of disorder, and an unflinching sense of public duty. Spenser's admiration of him was sincere and earnest. In his case the allegory almost becomes history. Arthur, Lord Grey, is Sir Arthegal, the Knight of Justice. The story touches apparently on some passages of his career, when his dislike of the French marriage placed him in opposition to the Queen, and even for a time threw him with the supporters of Mary. But the adventures of Arthegal mainly preserve the memory of Lord Grey's terrible exploits against wrong and rebellion in Ireland. These exploits are represented in the doings of the iron man Talus, his squire, with his destroying flail, swift, irresistible, inexorable ; a figure, borrowed and altered, after Spenser's wont, from a Greek legend. His overthrow of insolent giants, his annihilation of swarming "rascal routs," idealize and glorify that unrelenting policy, of which, though condemned in England, Spenser continued to be the advocate. In the story of Arthegal, long separated by undeserved misfortunes from the favour of the armed lady, Britomart, the virgin champion of right, of whom he was so worthy, doomed in spite of his honours to an early death, and assailed on his return from his victorious service by the furious insults of envy and malice, Spenser portrays almost without a veil, the hard fate of the unpopular patron whom he to the last defended and honoured.

Ralegh, his last protector, the Shepherd of the Ocean, to whose judgment he referred the work of his life, and under whose guidance he once more tried the quicksands of the Court, belonged to a different class from Sidney or Lord Grey ; but of his own class he

was the consummate and matchless example. He had
not Sidney's fine enthusiasm and nobleness; he had not
either Sidney's affectations. He had not Lord Grey's
single-minded hatred of wrong. He was a man to whom
his own interests were much; he was unscrupulous; he
was ostentatious; he was not above stooping to mean,
unmanly compliances with the humours of the Queen.
But he was a man with a higher ideal than he attempted
to follow. He saw, not without cynical scorn, through
the shows and hollowness of the world. His intellect
was of that clear and unembarrassed power which takes
in as wholes things which other men take in part by part.
And he was in its highest form a representative of that
spirit of adventure into the unknown and the wonderful
of which Drake was the coarser and rougher example,
realizing in serious earnest, on the sea and in the New
World, the life of knight-errantry feigned in romances.
With Ralegh, as with Lord Grey, Spenser comes to
history; and he even seems to have been moved, as the
poem went on, partly by pity, partly by amusement, to
shadow forth in his imaginary world, not merely Ralegh's
brilliant qualities, but also his frequent misadventures and
mischances in his career at Court. Of all her favourites
Ralegh was the one whom his wayward mistress seemed
to find most delight in tormenting. The offence which
he gave by his secret marriage suggested the scenes
describing the utter desolation of Prince Arthur's squire,
Timias, at the jealous wrath of the Virgin Huntress,
Belphœbe,—scenes, which extravagant as they are, can
hardly be called a caricature of Ralegh's real behaviour
in the Tower in 1593. But Spenser is not satisfied with
this one picture. In the last Book Timias appears again,
the victim of slander and ill-usage, even after he had

recovered Belphœbe's favour; he is baited like a wild
bull, by mighty powers of malice, falsehood, and calumny;
he is wounded by the tooth of the Blatant Beast; and
after having been cured, not without difficulty, and not
without significant indications on the part of the poet that
his friend had need to restrain and chasten his unruly
spirit, he is again delivered over to an ignominious
captivity, and the insults of Disdain and Scorn.

> Then up he made him rise, and forward fare,
> Led in a rope which both his hands did bynd;
> Ne ought that foole for pity did him spare,
> But with his whip, him following behynd,
> Him often scourg'd, and forst his feete to fynd:
> And other-whiles with bitter mockes and mowes
> He would him scorne, that to his gentle mynd
> Was much more grievous then the others blowes:
> Words sharpely wound, but greatest griefe of scorning
>   growes.

Spenser knew Ralegh only in the promise of his
adventurous prime—so buoyant and fearless, so inexhaustible in project and resource, so unconquerable by
checks and reverses. The gloomier portion of Ralegh's
career was yet to come : its intrigues, its grand yet really
gambling and unscrupulous enterprises, the long years
of prison and authorship, and its not unfitting close, in
the English statesman's death by the headsman—so tranquil though violent, so ceremoniously solemn, so composed, so dignified;—such a contrast to all other forms
of capital punishment, then or since.

Spenser has been compared to Pindar, and contrasted
with Cervantes. The contrast, in point of humour, and
the truth that humour implies, is favourable to the
Spaniard : in point of moral earnestness and sense of
poetic beauty, to the Englishman. What Cervantes only

thought ridiculous Spenser used, and not in vain, for a
high purpose. The ideas of knight-errantry were really
more absurd than Spenser allowed himself to see. But
that idea of the gentleman which they suggested, that
picture of human life as a scene of danger, trial, effort,
defeat, recovery, which they lent themselves to image
forth, was more worth insisting on, than the exposure of
their folly and extravagance. There was nothing to be
made of them, Cervantes thought ; and nothing to be
done, but to laugh off what they had left, among living
Spaniards, of pompous imbecility or mistaken pretensions.
Spenser, knowing that they must die, yet believed that
out of them might be raised something nobler and more
real, enterprise, duty, resistance to evil, refinement, hatred
of the mean and base. The energetic and high-reaching
manhood which he saw in the remarkable personages
round him he shadowed forth in the *Faery Queen.* He
idealized the excellences and the trials of this first generation of English gentlemen, as Bunyan afterwards idealized the piety, the conflicts, and the hopes of Puritan
religion.   Neither were universal types ; neither were
perfect. The manhood in which Spenser delights, with
all that was admirable and attractive in it, had still
much of boyish incompleteness and roughness : it had
noble aims, it had generosity, it had loyalty, it had a very
real reverence for purity and religion ; but it was young
in experience of a new world, it was wanting in self-
mastery, it was often pedantic and self-conceited ; it was
an easier prey than it ought to have been to discreditable
temptations. And there is a long interval between any
of Spenser's superficial and thin conceptions of character,
and such deep and subtle creations as Hamlet or Othello,
just as Bunyan's strong but narrow ideals of religion,

true as they are up to a certain point, fall short of the
length and breadth and depth of what Christianity has
made of man, and may yet make of him. But in the
ways which Spenser chose, he will always delight and
teach us. The spectacle of what is heroic and self-
devoted, of honour for principle and truth, set before
us with so much insight and sympathy, and combined
with so much just and broad observation on those
accidents and conditions of our mortal state which touch
us all, will never appeal to English readers in vain, till
we have learned a new language, and adopted new canons
of art, of taste, and of morals. It is not merely that he
has left imperishable images which have taken their place
among the consecrated memorials of poetry and the household thoughts of all cultivated men. But he has per-
manently lifted the level of English poetry by a great
and sustained effort of rich and varied art, in which one
main purpose rules, loyalty to what is noble and pure,
and in which this main purpose subordinates to itself
every feature and every detail, and harmonizes some that
by themselves seem least in keeping with it.

CHAPTER VI.

THE publication of the *Faery Queen* in 1590 had made
the new poet of the *Shepherd's Calendar* a famous man.
He was no longer merely the favourite of a knot of
enthusiastic friends, and outside of them only recognized and valued at his true measure by such judges as
Sidney and Ralegh.   By the common voice of all the
poets of his time he was now acknowledged as the first of
living English poets.   It is not easy for us, who live in
these late times and are familiar with so many literary mas-
terpieces, to realize the surprise of a first and novel achievement in literature ; the effect on an age, long and eagerly
seeking after poetical expression, of the appearance at last
of a work of such power, richness, and finished art.

It can scarcely be doubted, I think, from the bitter
sarcasms interspersed in his later poems, that Spenser
expected more from his triumph than it brought him.
It opened no way of advancement for him in England.
He continued for a while in that most ungrateful and
unsatisfactory employment, the service of the State in
Ireland ; and that he relinquished in 1593.[5]   At the end

---

[5] Who is *Edmondus Spenser, Prebendary of Effin* (Elphin) ? in
a list of arrears of first fruits ; Calendar of State Papers, *Ireland,*

of 1591 he was again at Kilcolman. He had written and probably sent to Ralegh, though he did not publish it till 1595, the record already quoted of the last two year's events, *Colin Clout's come home again,*—his visit, under Ralegh's guidance, to the Court, his thoughts and recollections of its great ladies, his generous criticisms on poets, the people and courtiers whom he had seen and heard of; how he had been dazzled, how he had been disenchanted, and how he was come home to his Irish mountains and streams and lakes, to enjoy their beauty, though in a "salvage" and "foreign" land; to find in this peaceful and tranquil retirement something far better than the heat of ambition and the intrigues of envious rivalries; and to contrast with the profanations of the name of love which had disgusted him in a dissolute society, the higher and purer ideal of it which he could honour and pursue in the simplicity of his country life.

And in Ireland, the rejected adorer of the Rosalind of the *Shepherd's Calendar* found another and still more perfect Rosalind, who, though she was at first inclined to repeat the cruelty of the earlier one, in time relented, and received such a dower of poetic glory as few poets have bestowed upon their brides. It has always appeared strange that Spenser's passion for the first Rosalind should have been so lasting, that in his last pastoral, *Colin Clout's come home again,* written so late as 1591, and published after he was married, he should end his poem by reverting to this long-past love passage, defending her on the ground of her incomparable excellence

Dec. 8, 1586, p. 222. Church preferments were under special circumstances allowed to be held by laymen. See the Queen's "Instructions," 1579; in Preface to Calendar of Carew MSS. 1589—1600, p. ci.

and his own unworthiness, against the blame of friendly
"shepherds," witnesses of the "languors of his too long
dying," and angry with her hard-heartedness. It may be
that, according to Spenser's way of making his masks and
figures suggest but not fully express their antitypes,[2]
Rosalind here bears the image of the real mistress of this
time, the "country lass," the Elizabeth of the sonnets,
who was, in fact, for a while as unkind as the earlier
Rosalind. The history of this later wooing, its hopes and
anguish, its varying currents, its final unexpected success,
is the subject of a collection of Sonnets, which have the
disadvantage of provoking comparison with the Sonnets of
Shakespere. There is no want in them of grace and sweetness, and they ring true with genuine feeling and warm
affection, though they have of course their share of the
conceits then held proper for love poems. But they
want the power and fire, as well as the perplexing mys-
tery, of those of the greater master. His bride was also
immortalized as a fourth among the three Graces, in a
richly-painted passage in the last book of the *Faery
Queen*. But the most magnificent tribute to her is the
great Wedding Ode, the *Epithalamion*, the finest composition of its kind, probably, in any language : so im-
petuous and unflagging, so orderly and yet so rapid in
the onward march of its stately and varied stanzas ; so
passionate, so flashing with imaginative wealth, yet so
refined and self-restrained. It was always easy for Spenser
to open the floodgates of his inexhaustible fancy. With
him,—

The numbers flow as fast as spring doth rise.

[2] "In these kind of historical allusions Spenser usually per-
plexes the subject : he leads you on, and then designedly misleads
you."—Upton, quoted by Craik, iii. 92.

But here he has thrown into his composition all his power
of concentration, of arrangement, of strong and harmonious
government over thought and image, over language and
measure and rhythm ; and the result is unquestionably
one of the grandest lyrics in English poetry.   We have
learned to think the subject unfit for such free poetical
treatment ; Spenser's age did not.

Of the lady of whom all this was said, and for whom all
this was written, the family name has not been thought
worth preserving.   We know that by her Christian name
she was a namesake of the great queen, and of Spenser's
mother.   She is called a country lass, which may mean
anything ; and the marriage appears to have been solem-
nized in Cork, on what was then Midsummer Day, " Barnaby the Bright," the day when " the sun is in his cheerful
height," June $\frac{11}{22}$, 1594.   Except that she survived Spenser,
that she married again, and had some legal quarrels with
one of her own sons about his lands, we know nothing
more about her.   Of two of the children whom she brought
him, the names have been preserved, and they indicate that
in spite of love and poetry, and the charms of Kilcolman,
Spenser felt as Englishmen feel in Australia or in India.
To call one of them *Sylvanus,* and the other *Peregrine,*
reveals to us that Ireland was still to him a " salvage land,"
and he a pilgrim and stranger in it ; as Moses called his
firstborn Gershom, a strangèr here—" for he said, I have
been a stranger in a strange land."

In the year after his marriage, he sent over these
memorials of it to be published in London, and they were
entered at Stationers' Hall in November, 1595.   The same
year he came over himself, bringing with him the second
instalment of the *Faery Queen,* which was entered for
publication the following January, 159$\frac{5}{6}$.   Thus the half

of the projected work was finished ; and finished, as
we know from one of the Sonnets (80), before his
marriage. After his long "race through Fairy land," he
asks leave to rest, and solace himself with his "love's
sweet praise ; " and then " as a steed refreshed after toil,"
he will "stoutly that second worke assoyle." The first six
books were published together in 1596. He remained
most of the year in London, during which *The Four
Hymns on Love and Beauty, Earthly and Heavenly*, were
published ; and also a Dirge (*Daphnaida*) on Douglas
Howard, the wife of Arthur Gorges, the spirited narrator
of the Island Voyage of Essex and Ralegh, written in
1591 ; and a "spousal verse" (*Prothalamion*), on the
marriage of the two daughters of the Earl of Worcester,
late in 1596. But he was only a visitor in London.
The *Prothalamion* contains a final record of his dis-
appointments in England.

> I, (whom sullein care,
> Through discontent of my long fruitlesse stay
> In Princes Court, and expectation vayne
> Of idle hopes, which still doe fly away,
> Like empty shaddowes, did afflict my brayne,)
> Walkt forth to ease my payne
> Along the shoare of silver streaming Themmes—

His marriage ought to have made him happy. He professed to find the highest enjoyment in the quiet and
retirement of country life. He was in the prime of life,
successful beyond all his fellows in his special work, and
apparently with unabated interest in what remained to be
done of it. And though he could not but feel himself
at a distance from the "sweet civility " of England, and
socially at disadvantage compared to those whose lines
had fallen to them in its pleasant places, yet nature,

which he loved so well, was still friendly to him, if men
were wild and dangerous. He is never weary of praising
the natural advantages of Ireland.   Speaking of the
North, he says,—

> And sure it is yet a most beautifull and sweet countrey as
> any is under heaven, seamed throughout with many goodly
> rivers, replenished with all sortes of fish, most aboundantly
> sprinckled with many sweet Ilandes, and goodly lakes, like litle
> Inland Seas, that will carry even ships upon theyr waters,
> adorned with goodly woodes fitt for building of howses and
> shippes, soe comodiously, as that yf some princes in the world
> had them, they would soone hope to be lordes of all the seas,
> and ere long of all the world; also full of good portes and
> havens opening upon England and Scotland, as inviting us to
> come to them, to see what excellent comodityes that countrey
> can affoord, besides the soyle it self most fertile, fitt to yeeld
> all kind of fruite that shal be comitted therunto.   And lastly,
> the heavens most milde and temperat, though somewhat more
> moyst then the part toward the West.

His own home at Kilcolman charmed and delighted
him.   It was not his fault that its trout streams, its Mulla
and Fanchin, are not as famous as Walter Scott's Teviot
and Tweed, or Wordsworth's Yarrow and Duddon, or
that its hills, Old Mole, and Arlo Hill, have not kept a
poetic name like Helvellyn and " Eildon's triple height."
They have failed to become familiar names to us.   But the
beauties of his home inspired more than one sweet pastoral picture in the *Faery Queen ;* and in the last fragment remaining to us of it, he celebrates his mountains
and woods and valleys as once the fabled resort of the
Divine Huntress and her Nymphs, and the meeting-place
of the Gods.

There was one drawback to the enjoyment of his Irish
country life, and of the natural attractiveness of Kilcolman.

" Who knows not Arlo Hill?" he exclaims, in the scene
just referred to from the fragment on *Mutability*.
"Arlo, the best and fairest hill in all the holy island's
heights." It was well known to all Englishmen who had
to do with the South of Ireland. How well it was known
in the Irish history of the time, may be seen in the
numerous references to it, under various forms, such as
Aharlo, Harlow, in the Index to the Irish Calendar of
Papers of this troublesome date, and to continual encounters and ambushes in its notoriously dangerous woods.
He means by it the highest part of the Galtee range,
below which to the north, through a glen or defile, runs
the "river Aherlow." Galtymore, the summit, rises, with
precipice and gully, more than 3000 feet, above the plains
of Tipperary, and is seen far and wide. It was connected
with the "great wood," the wild region of forest, mountain,
and bog which stretched half across Munster from the Suir
to the Shannon. It was the haunt and fastness of Irish out-
lawry and rebellion in the South, which so long sheltered
Desmond and his followers. Arlo and its "fair forests,"
harbouring "thieves and wolves," was an uncomfortable
neighbour to Kilcolman. The poet describes it as ruined
by a curse pronounced on the lovely land by the offended
goddess of the Chase, —

Which too too true that land's in-dwellers since have found.

He was not only living in an insecure part, on the very
border of disaffection and disturbance, but like every
Englishman living in Ireland, he was living amid ruins.
An English home in Ireland, however fair, was a home on
the sides of Ætna or Vesuvius : it stood where the lava
flood had once passed, and upon not distant fires. Spenser
has left us his thoughts on the condition of Ireland, in a
paper written between the two rebellions, some time be-

tween 1595 and 1598, after the twelve or thirteen years of
so-called peace which followed the overthrow of Desmond,
and when Tyrone's rebellion was becoming serious. It
seems to have been much copied in manuscript, but though
entered for publication in 1598, it was not printed till long
after his death in 1633. A copy of it among the Irish papers
of 1598 shows that it had come under the eyes of the
English Government. It is full of curious observations, of
shrewd political remarks, of odd and confused ethnography;
but more than all this, it is a very vivid and impressive
picture of what Sir Walter Ralegh called " the common
woe of Ireland." It is a picture of a noble realm, which
its inhabitants and its masters did not know what to do
with ; a picture of hopeless mistakes, misunderstandings,
misrule ; a picture of piteous misery and suffering on the
part of a helpless and yet untameable and mischievous
population—of unrelenting and scornful rigour on the part
of their stronger rulers, which yet was absolutely ineffec-
tual to reclaim or subdue them.   " Men of great wisdom,"
Spenser writers, " have often wished that all that land
were a sea-pool." Everything, people thought, had been
tried, and tried in vain.

Marry, soe there have beene divers good plottes and wise
counsells cast alleready about reformation of that realme; but
they say, it is the fatall desteny of that land, that noe purposes,
whatsoever are meant for her good, will prosper or take good
effect, which, whether it proceede from the very GENIUS of the
soyle, or influence of the starres, or that Allmighty God hath
not yet appoynted the time of her reformation, or that He
reserveth her in this unquiett state still for some secrett
scourdge, which shall by her come unto England, it is hard to
be knowen, but yet much to be feared.

The unchanging fatalities of Ireland appear in Spenser's
account in all their well-known forms ; some of them, as if

they were what we were reading of yesterday. Throughout the work there is a honest zeal for order, an honest
hatred of falsehood, sloth, treachery, and disorder. But
there does not appear a trace of consideration for what
the Irish might feel or desire or resent. He is sen-
sible indeed of English mismanagement and vacillation,
of the way in which money and force were wasted by
not being boldly and intelligently employed; he enlarges
on that power of malignity and detraction which he has
figured in the Blatant Beast of the *Faery Queen*: but of
English cruelty, of English injustice, of English rapa-
city, of English prejudice, he is profoundly unconscious.
He only sees that things are getting worse and more dangerous; and though he, like others, has his "plot" for the
subjugation and pacification of the island, and shrinks
from nothing in the way of severity, not even, if necessary, from extermination, his outlook is one of deep despair.
He calculates the amount of force, of money, of time,
necessary to break down all resistance : he is minute and
perhaps skilful in building his forts and disposing his
garrisons; he is very earnest about the necessity of cut-
ting broad roads through the woods, and building bridges
in place of fords; he contemplates restored churches,
parish schools, a better order of clergy. But where the
spirit was to come from of justice, of conciliation, of steady
and firm resistance to corruption and selfishness, he gives
us no light. What it comes to is, that with patience,
temper, and public spirit, Ireland might be easily reformed
and brought into order : but unless he hoped for patience,
temper, and public spirit from Lord Essex, to whom he
seems to allude as the person "on whom the eye of England is fixed, and our last hopes now rest," he too easily
took for granted what was the real difficulty. His picture

is exact and forcible, of one side of the truth ; it seems
beyond the thought of an honest, well-informed, and
noble-minded Englishman that there was another side.
But he was right in his estimate of the danger, and
of the immediate evils which produced it. He was
right in thinking that want of method, want of control,
want of confidence, and an untimely parsimony, prevented
severity from having a fair chance of preparing a platform
for reform and conciliation. He was right in his convic-
tion of the inveterate treachery of the Irish Chiefs, partly
the result of ages of mismanagement, but now incurable.
While he was writing, Tyrone, a craftier and bolder man
than Desmond, was taking up what Desmond had failed
in. He was playing a game with the English authorities
which as things then were is almost beyond belief. He was
outwitting or cajoling the veterans of Irish government,
who knew perfectly well what he was, and yet let him
amuse them with false expectations—men like Sir John
Norreys, who broke his heart when he found out how
Tyrone had baffled and made a fool of him. Wishing to
gain time for help from Spain, and to extend the rebellion,
he revolted, submitted, sued for pardon but did not care
to take it when granted, fearlessly presented himself
before the English officers while he was still beleaguer-
ing their posts, led the English forces a chase through
mountains and bogs, inflicted heavy losses on them,
and yet managed to keep negotiations open as long as
it suited him. From 1594 to 1598, the rebellion
had been gaining ground ; it had crept round from
Ulster to Connaught, from Connaught to Leinster, and
now from Connaught to the borders of Munster. But
Munster, with its English landlords and settlers, was still
on the whole quiet. At the end of 1597, the Council at

Dublin reported home that "Munster was the best tempered of all the rest at this present time ; for that though not long since sundry loose persons " (among them the base sons of Lord Roche, Spenser's adversary in land suits) "became Robin Hoods and slew some of the undertakers; dwelling scattered in thatched houses and remote places near to woods and fastnesses, yet now they are cut off, and no known disturbers left who are like to make any dangerous alteration on the sudden." But they go on to add that they " have intelligence that many are practised withal from the North, to be of combination with the rest, and stir coals in Munster, whereby the whole realm might be in a general uproar." And they repeat their opinion that they must be prepared for a " universal Irish war, intended to shake off all English government."

In April, 1598, Tyrone received a new pardon ; in the following August, he surprised an English army near Armagh, and shattered it with a defeat, the bloodiest and most complete ever received by the English in Ireland. Then the storm burst. Tyrone sent a force into Munster : and once more Munster rose. It was a rising of the dispossessed proprietors and the whole native population against the English undertakers ; a " ragged number of rogues and boys," as the English Council describes them ; rebel kernes, pouring out of the "great wood,"and from Arlo, the " chief fastness of the rebels." Even the chiefs, usually on good terms with the English, could not resist the stream. Even Thomas Norreys, the President, was surprised, and retired to Cork, bringing down on himself a severe reprimand from the English Government. " You might better have resisted than you did, considering the many defensible houses and castles possessed by the undertakers, who, for aught we can hear, were by no means com-

forted nor supported by you, but either from lack of comfort from you, or out of mere cowardice, fled away from
the rebels on the first alarm." "Whereupon," says Cox,
the Irish historian, "the Munsterians, generally, rebel in
October, and kill, murder, ravish and spoil without mercy ;
and Tyrone made James Fitz-Thomas, Earl of Desmond,
on condition to be tributary to him; he was the hand-
somest man of his time, and is commonly called the *Sugan*
Earl."

On the last day of the previous September (Sept. 30,
1598), the English Council had written to the Irish
Government to appoint Edmund Spenser, Sheriff of the
County of Cork, "a gentleman dwelling in the County
of Cork, who is so well known unto you all for his good
and commendable parts, being a man endowed with good
knowledge in learning, and not unskilful or without
experience in the wars."   In October, Munster was in the
hands of the insurgents, who were driving Norreys before
them, and sweeping out of house and castle the panic-
stricken English settlers.   On December 9th, Norreys
wrote home a despatch about the state of the province.
This despatch was sent to England by Spenser, as we
learn from a subsequent despatch of Norreys of December
21.[3]   It was received at Whitehall, as appears from Robert
Cecil's endorsement, on the 24th of December. The passage
from Ireland seems to have been a long one.   And this is
the last original document which remains about Spenser.

What happened to him in the rebellion we learn generally from two sources, from Camden's *History*, and from
Drummond of Hawthornden's Recollections of Ben Jon-

------

[3] I am indebted for this reference to Mr. Hans Claude Hamilton.
See also his Preface to Calendar of Irish Papers, 1574-85, p.
lxxvi.

son's conversations with him in 1619. In the Munster insurrection of October, the new Earl of Desmond's followers did not forget that Kilcolman was an old possession of the Desmonds. It was sacked and burnt. Jonson related that a little new-born child of Spenser's perished in the flames. Spenser and his wife escaped, and he came over to England, a ruined and heart-broken man. He died Jan. 16, 159⅘; "he died," said Jonson, "for lack of bread in King Street [Westminster], and refused twenty pieces sent to him by my Lord of Essex, saying that he had no time to spend them." He was buried in the Abbey, near the grave of Chaucer, and his funeral was at the charge of the Earl of Essex. Beyond this we know nothing ; nothing about the details of his escape, nothing of the fate of his manuscripts, or the condition in which he left his work, nothing about the suffering he went through in England, All conjecture is idle waste of time. We only know that the first of English poets perished miserably and prematurely, one of the many heavy sacrifices which the evil fortune of Ireland has cost to England ; one of many illustrious victims to the madness, the evil customs, the vengeance of an ill-treated and ill-governed people.

One Irish rebellion brought him to Ireland, another drove him out of it. Desmond's brought him to pass his life there, and to fill his mind with the images of what was then Irish life, with its scenery, its antipathies, its tempers, its chances, and necessities. Tyrone's swept him from Ireland, beggared and hopeless. Ten years after his death, a bookseller, reprinting the six books of the *Faery Queen*, added two cantos and a fragment, *On Mutability*, supposed to be part of the *Legend of Constancy*. Where and how he got them he has not

told us. It is a strange and solemn meditation, on
the universal subjection of all things to the inexorable
conditions of change. It is strange, with its odd episode
and fable which Spenser cannot resist about his neighbouring streams, its borrowings from Chaucer, and its quaint
mixture of mythology with sacred and with Irish scenery,
Olympus and Tabor, and his own rivers and mountains.
But it is full of his power over thought and imagery ; and
it is quite in a different key from anything in the first six
books. It has an undertone of awe-struck and pathetic
sadness.

> What man that sees the ever whirling wheel
> Of Change, the which all mortal things doth sway,
> But that thereby doth find and plainly feel
> How Mutability in them doth play
> Her cruel sports to many men's decay.

He imagines a mighty Titaness, sister of Hecate and
Bellona, most beautiful and most terrible, who challenges
universal dominion over all things in earth and heaven, sun
and moon, planets and stars, times and seasons, life and
death ; and finally over the wills and thoughts and
natures of the gods, even of Jove himself ; and who
pleads her cause before the awful Mother of all things,
figured as Chaucer had already imagined her :—

> Great Nature, ever young, yet full of eld ;
> Still moving, yet unmoved from her stead ;
> Unseen of any, yet of all beheld,
> Thus sitting on her throne.

He imagines all the powers of the upper and nether worlds
assembled before her on his own familiar hills, instead of
Olympus, where she shone like the Vision which "dazed"
those "three sacred saints" on "Mount Thabor." Before
her pass all things known of men, in rich and picturesque
procession ; the Seasons pass, and the Months, and the

Hours, and Day and Night, Life, as "a fair young lusty boy," Death, grim and grisly ;—

> Yet is he nought but parting of the breath,
> Ne ought to see, but like a shade to weene,
> Unbodied, unsoul'd, unheard, unseene—

and on all of them the claims of the Titaness, Mutability, are acknowledged. Nothing escapes her sway in this present state, except Nature which, while seeming to change, never really changes her ultimate constituent elements, or her universal laws. But when she seemed to have extorted the admission of her powers, Nature silences her. Change is apparent, and not real ; and the time is coming when all change shall end in the final changeless change.

> " I well consider all that ye have said,
> And find that all things stedfastnesse do hate
> And changed be ; yet, being rightly wayd,
> They are not changed from their first estate ;
> But by their change their being do dilate,
> And turning to themselves at length againe,
> Do worke their owne perfection so by fate :
> Then over them Change doth not rule and raigne,
> But they raigne over Change, and do their states maintaine.
>
> " Cease therefore, daughter, further to aspire,
> And thee content thus to be rul'd by mee,
> For thy decay thou seekst by thy desire ;
> But time shall come that all shall changed bee,
> And from thenceforth none no more change shal see."
> So was the Titanesse put downe and whist,
> And Jove confirm'd in his imperiall see.
> Then was that whole assembly quite dismist,
> And Natur's selfe did vanish, whither no man wist.

What he meant—how far he was thinking of those daring arguments of religious and philosophical change of which the world was beginning to be full, we cannot now tell.

The allegory was not finished : at least it is lost to us. We have but a fragment more, the last fragment of his poetry. It expresses the great commonplace which so impressed itself on the men of that time, and of which his works are full. No words could be more appropriate to be the last words of one who was so soon to be in his own person such an instance of their truth. They are fit closing words to mark his tragic and pathetic disappearance from the high and animated scene in which his imagination worked. And they record, too, the yearning hope of rest not extinguished by terrible and fatal disaster :—

> When I bethinke me on that speech whyleare
> Of Mutabilitie, and well it way,
> Me seemes, that though she all unworthy were
> Of the Heav'ns Rule ; yet, very sooth to say,
> In all things else she beares the greatest sway :
> Which makes me loath this state of life so tickle,
> And love of things so vaine to cast away ;
> Whose flowring pride, so fading and so fickle,
> Short Time shall soon cut down with his consuming
> sickle.
>
> Then gin I thinke on that which Nature sayd,
> Of that same time when no more Change shall be,
> But stedfast rest of all things, firmely stayd
> Upon the pillours of Eternity,
> That is contrayr to Mutabilitie;
> For all that moveth doth in Change delight :
> But thence-forth all shall rest eternally
> With Him that is the God of Sabaoth hight :
> O ! that great Sabaoth God, grant me that Sabaoths
> sight.

THE END.

LONDON :
GILBERT AND RIVINGTON, PRINTERS,
ST. JOHN'S SQUARE.

For EU product safety concerns, contact us at Calle de José Abascal, 56–1°,
28003 Madrid, Spain or eugpsr@cambridge.org.

.

www.ingramcontent.com/pod-product-compliance
Ingram Content Group UK Ltd.
Pitfield, Milton Keynes, MK11 3LW, UK
UKHW012344130625
459647UK00009B/514